Madison's Battery Workers
1934-1952
A History of
Federal Labor
Union 19587

ROBERT H. ZIEGER

ILR Paperback No. 16

NEW YORK STATE SCHOOL OF
INDUSTRIAL & LABOR RELATIONS
CORNELL UNIVERSITY

1977

Library of Congress Catalog Number: 77-1530
ISBN: 0-87546-062-3
ISSN: 0070-0177

Price: $4.50, paperbound

Order from
Publications Division
New York State School of Industrial and Labor Relations
Cornell University, Box 1000
Ithaca, New York 14853

Library of Congress Cataloging in Publication Data

Zieger, Robert H.
    Madison's battery workers, 1934–1952.

    (ILR paperback; no. 16)
    Bibliography: p.
    Includes index.
    1. Ray-O-Vac Federal Union No. 19587, Madison, Wis. —
History. I. Title. II. Series.
HD6515.B352M338   331.88'12'1350977584   77-1530
ISBN 0-87546-062-3 pbk.

*Cover photo courtesy of State Historical
Society of Wisconsin.*

Contents

For my wife, Gay Pitman Zieger

Preface

In the spring of 1972, I read through the records of hundreds of federal labor unions in the Strikes and Agreements Files of the American Federation of Labor (AFL) Papers at the State Historical Society of Wisconsin in Madison. During that spring and summer I also examined the records of the AFL proper as well as those of several prominent international unions and the papers of leading figures in the labor movement of the 1930s and 1940s. My research took me to West Virginia University, Catholic University, Pennsylvania State University, and Wayne State University. On a later trip I worked with archival material in Washington, D.C., and Suitland, Maryland, as well as with additional AFL-CIO materials in the headquarters building in Washington.

Through this research the events of the thirties and forties took on new dimensions. Correspondence, reports, and memoirs brought vividly to life the struggle for industrial unionism, the birth pangs of the CIO, the bitterness of the AFL-CIO split, and the many sharp and even bloody battles of this turbulent era.

Although few of the federal labor unions (FLUs) were directly involved in these heroic events, I was fascinated by the sporadic record of tens of thousands of men and women who were taking their first steps toward organization. In these deceptively prosaic local union records there seemed to be an important story, an integral part of the rise of American labor, that needed to be told. At the same time, these records were so spotty that there appeared to be no way to construct a coherent account of the activities of these unions. One could catch a glimpse of thousands of casket makers, beet sugar workers, pen and pencil makers, and dry cell battery operatives beginning to organize and to find a collective voice, but one could not follow their course or observe their triumphs and setbacks.

Fortunately, the State Historical Society houses records of Wisconsin local unions in addition to these AFL materials. In examining some of these, I learned that Federal Labor Union 19587, which represented production workers at the Ray-O-Vac Battery factory in Madison, had deposited a complete set of records, including correspondence and minute books, at the Society. These materials showed the daily concerns of the battery workers, and I began to grasp the relationship between general themes in the labor history of this period and the life of a local union. The records in the AFL files provided a broad, fragmentary overview; those in the files of FLU 19587 offered an opportunity for sharper focus.

I later discovered that Ray-O-Vac had sponsored an employee association in the 1920s and eagerly read through the microfilm copy of its newspaper. Unfortunately, neither the company nor, at first, the union was particularly eager to cooperate with me in uncovering additional material. Still, research for another topic in Washington in the summer of 1974 yielded additional material about 19587. Then a chance conversation spurred me to arrange interviews with veterans of the union's early years. This new information, together with ongoing research into more general themes of the 1930s and 1940s, encouraged me to put together a general knowledge of labor organization, broad impressions of the federal labor unions, and a more intimate understanding of the development of FLU 19587. In doing so, I have tried to avoid both esoteric local detail and flatulent abstraction. My aim has been to capture something of the human reality of one group of workers while at the same time illuminating broader patterns of labor activism.

Acknowledgments .

Throughout the preparation of this work, Barbara Hudy Bartkowiak served as my assistant. She arranged for the interviews, helped with research, and displayed an enthusiastic interest far beyond the call of duty. Her aid was essential. State Senator William Bablitch helped to secure the cooperation of the United Automobile Workers and the Wisconsin State AFL-CIO; his hospitality made my interviewing sojourn to Madison both pleasant and productive. William Troestler of the Milwaukee UAW office and Maxine Boylan, secretary of UAW Local 1329, assisted in contacting veteran members of Federal Labor Union 19587. Harold J. "Red" Newton of the Wisconsin State AFL-CIO Public Relations office helped put me in touch with others whom I interviewed, answered questions patiently, and provided important printed materials. Gregory Wallig, in addition to granting an interview, provided documentary materials unavailable elsewhere.

Josephine Harper and Kay Thompson, of the Manuscripts Division of the State Historical Society of Wisconsin, and Art Fish of the University of Wisconsin—Stevens Point Library facilitated my research. Daniel Goggin and Janet Hargett of the National Archives helped in securing government records. Melodie Rue of the Iconographic Collection of the State Historical Society of Wisconsin found the cover photograph after much diligent searching. Professors Burton I. Kaufman of Kansas State University and D. Le Roy Ashby of Washington State University read an earlier version of this work, as did Professor Emeritus A. Bower Sageser of Kansas State University. Each provided valuable commentary; none bears any responsibility for its remaining flaws. Frances Benson improved the manuscript with sound editorial guidance.

A Teacher Improvement Leave at the University of Wisconsin—Stevens Point, together with grants from the Board of General Research at Kansas State University, the American

Philosophical Society, and the National Endowment for the Humanities, supported my research.

I owe a special debt to Byron Buchholz, Elmer Davis, Evelyn Gotzion, Mrs. Lawrence Grab, Pat Lowe, Max Onsager, Marion Shaw, David Sigman, William Skaar, Mr. and Mrs. John Stromski, and Gregory Wallig, all of whom patiently answered my questions, displayed warm hospitality, and otherwise helped a wandering scholar. My wife, Gay Pitman Zieger, despite her own heavy schedule, once again provided that indispensable mixture of encouragement and criticism. Finally, my thanks go to the men and women who created and maintained FLU 19587 down through the years and who—to paraphrase Yogi Berra—made this project necessary.

ROBERT H. ZIEGER

Manhattan, Kansas
November 1, 1976

Leading Personalities

Auringer, Myrna, *recording secretary, FLU 19587, 1930s*

Berigan, L. G., *Ray-O-Vac officer, 1920s–40s; production manager and vice-president during World War II*

Bidgood, Frank, *FLU 19587 activist, 1930s–40s; president, 1945*

Biemiller, Andrew, *Wisconsin State Federation of Labor (WSFL) organizer, 1932–42; member, Wisconsin state assembly, 1937–41; member, U.S. Congress, 1945–47, 1949–51; AFL lobbyist, 1952–56; legislative director, AFL-CIO, 1956–*

Breitzke, Al, *president, FLU 19587, 1939–43; member, Badger Lodge 1406, International Association of Machinists, 1945–*

Buchholz, Byron, *member, FLU 19587, 1935–50s; recording secretary, 1945*

Cargill, W. W., *president, Ray-O-Vac, 1934–47; chairman of the board, 1947–52*

Clark, Nathaniel, *member, Regional Labor Board of National Labor Relations Board; assisted in settlement of 1936 Ray-O-Vac dispute*

Davis, Elmer, *member, FLU 19587 and UAW Local 1329, 1948–   ; president, UAW Local 1329, 1970s*

Edwards, Edward E., *secretary, Wisconsin FLU steering committee, ca. 1946–48*

Friedrick, Jacob F., *WSFL organizer; regional director, 1945–51; general secretary, Federated Trades Council, Milwaukee, 1951–59; general secretary, AFL-CIO Council, Milwaukee, 1959–69; chairman, Board of Regents, University of Wisconsin, 1961, 1962*

Garrison, Lloyd K., *chairman, National Labor Relations Board, 1934; dean, University of Wisconsin Law School, 1930s*

Gotzion, Evelyn, *member, FLU 19587 and UAW Local 1329, 1935–   ; shop steward, Grievance Committee member, delegate to state FLU conferences, 1930s–50s*

Grab, Iris (Mrs. Lawrence), *member, FLU 19587 and UAW Local 1329, 1942–73; president, FLU 19587, 1956 and after*

Haberman, George, *president, WSFL, 1934–66*

Hall, Ed, *UAW activist, 1930s; volunteer AFL organizer assisting FLU 19587, 1935*

Handley, J. J., *secretary-treasurer, WSFL, 1920s–30s*

Hein, Paul, *president, FLU 19587, 1943–44*

Herring, Emerold, *president, FLU 19587, 1944–45*

Heymanns, Charles, *AFL organizer, 1937–51; AFL regional director, 1951; AFL-CIO regional director, Region 12 (Wisconsin), 1955 and after*

Holmes, James P., *commissioner, United States Conciliation Service; assisted in Ray-O-Vac cases, 1941 and 1943*

Kastenbaum, Meyer, *chairman, tripartite panel, National War Labor Board, Region VI, Ray-O-Vac case, April–August 1943*

Kinney, Arvel W., *commissioner, United States Conciliation Service; assisted in Ray-O-Vac cases, 1946–47; vice-president, WSFL, 1955*

Lochner, Gerald, *FLU 19587 activist, 1935–39; president, 1936–39; chairman, Grievance Committee, 1939*

Lowe, Pat, *member, FLU 19587 and UAW Local 1329, 1934–68; member, Grievance Committee, ca. 1938–50*

Malcolm, Harry, *special representative on Ray-O-Vac case, National War Labor Board, March 1943*

McCutchin, William, *leading figure in founding of FLU 19587; president, 1934–36*

Mythen, Robert E., *commissioner, United States Conciliation Service; assisted in Ray-O-Vac disputes, 1935–36*

Ohl, Henry, Jr., *president, WSFL, 1917–40*

Onsager, Max, *FLU 19587 activist, 1934–63; member, Grievance Committee, ca. 1936–56; president, 1945–46*

Ramsay, J. B., *president, French Battery and Carbon Company, 1906–34*

Reist, Sol, *Madison AFL volunteer organizer, 1930s; assisted in founding of FLU 19587, 1934–35*

Saposs, David, *economist and labor expert, authority on federal labor unions*

Shaw, Marion, *member, FLU 19587 and UAW Local 1329, 1934–66*

Sigman, David, *member, Wisconsin state assembly, 1931 and after; AFL organizer, 1933–37; AFL regional director, 1937–45*

Skaar, William, *member, FLU 19587 and UAW Local 1329, 1934–70s; vice-president, 1936; member, Grievance Committee, 1936–39; president, 1938–39, 1946–56*

Stromski, John, *Ray-O-Vac machinist, 1941–70; member, FLU 19587, 1941–44; vice-president, 1944; member, Badger Lodge 1406, IAM, 1945–70*

Tyrell, D. W., *vice-president, Ray-O-Vac, 1940s; president, 1947 and after*

Uphoff, Walter, *WSFL organizer, 1940s; labor publicist and author*

Wallig, Gregory, *FLU 18456 activist, 1933–46; president, 1946–52; chairman, FLU Conference of Wisconsin, early 1950s; AFL representative, 1952–72*

Major Events

1906	French Battery and Carbon Company relocates in Madison
July 1919	French Battery and Carbon Company Employees' Association formed
June 16, 1933	National Industrial Recovery Act becomes law; Section 7 (a) spurs organization
1934	French Battery and Carbon Company name changed to Ray-O-Vac
May 9, 1934	Ray-O-Vac employees meet at Madison Labor Temple to form union
May 11, 1934	William McCutchin and other activists laid off
May 14, 1934	American Federation of Labor (AFL) grants federal charter 19587 to Ray-O-Vac employees
ca. July 1, 1934	McCutchin and other activists reinstated
July 5, 1935	National Labor Relations Act becomes law
October 1, 1935	Ray-O-Vac and FLU 19587 sign first agreement
October 18, 1935	John L. Lewis punches William Hutcheson at AFL convention, Atlantic City
November 9, 1935	Formation of Committee on Industrial Organization (CIO) within AFL
April 8–9, 1936	Firing of three workers, including union officers, precipitates crisis at Ray-O-Vac; strike vote taken
May 14, 1936	Agreement signed; strike does not occur

August 1936	CIO unions suspended by AFL Executive Council
December 31, 1936	United Auto Workers begin sit-down strike at Flint, Michigan; strike lasts until February 11, 1937
March 4, 1937	Ray-O-Vac and FLU 19587 sign first union shop contract
May 30, 1937	Memorial Day Massacre of steelworkers, Chicago
October 1937	William Skaar attends AFL convention, Denver; presses cause of federal labor unions
Fall 1938	Growing crisis in contract talks at Ray-O-Vac; company insists on wage cuts
December 10, 1938	Skaar resigns from Grievance Committee; elected president of FLU 19587
December 22, 1938	Ray-O-Vac closes down Madison operations; unionists charge lockout
February 24, 1939	New contract embodying 15 percent wage cuts ratified
December 1939	Skaar and Gerald Lochner leave Ray-O-Vac
December 1, 1939	Al Breitzke elected president of FLU 19587; reelected every year until 1943
July 1940	Skaar appointed safety director for Ray-O-Vac; serves in that capacity during World War II
December 7, 1941	Japanese attack on Pearl Harbor
December 17, 1941	Organized labor makes no-strike pledge
January 12, 1942	President Franklin D. Roosevelt creates National War Labor Board (NWLB)
December 22, 1942– May 3, 1943	Contract negotiations between Ray-O-Vac and FLU 19587; intervention in March by NWLB

May 10, 1943	Union ratifies agreement
August 6, 1943	NWLB reaffirms 19587's union shop
December 11, 1943	Paul Hein defeats Breitzke for presidency of FLU 19587
September 27, 1944	Hein resigns
December 9, 1944	Emerold Herring elected president of FLU 19587
Late 1944– early 1945	Toolroom and maintenance employees join Badger Lodge 1406, International Association of Machinists
February 10, 1945	Frank Bidgood elected president of FLU 19587
November 1945	UAW strikes General Motors; lasts 113 days
December 8, 1945	Max Onsager elected president of FLU 19587
February 1946	Postwar strikes reach peak; unprecedented 23 million man-days lost to strikes
March 20, 1946	FLU 19587 requests and receives strike sanction from AFL as negotiations bog down
May 9, 1946	FLU 19587 dispute settled without strike
August 1, 1946	Ray-O-Vac employees endorse union shop (500 to 11) in recertification election
December 1946	Skaar elected president of FLU 19587
April 12, 1947	After lengthy negotiations and strike vote, 19587 membership ratifies agreement with Ray-O-Vac
May 1947	Wisconsin FLU delegates appear before AFL Executive Council in Milwaukee to press for strengthening of federal unions in AFL
June 23, 1947	Labor-Management Relations Act becomes law

October 1947   FLU delegates at AFL convention seek
           strengthening of federal unions

October 1949   Wisconsin delegates lead efforts to enhance
           status of federal unions

October 1951   Wisconsin delegates renew efforts to upgrade
           federal unions at AFL convention

January 11, 1952 Gregory Wallig protests to William Green raid-
           ing of FLUs by national unions

December 1955   AFL and CIO merge

June 1956   Badger Lodge 1406 strikes Ray-O-Vac; FLU
           19587 honors picket line; strike lasts five weeks

April 1963   FLU 19587 gives up charter; becomes UAW
           Local 1329

September–
December 1963   Local 1329 strikes Ray-O-Vac

1968   Local 1329 strikes Ray-O-Vac; UAW leaves
           AFL-CIO

I.

The Battery Workers and American Labor History

In 1934, the employees at the Ray-O-Vac Battery plant in Madison, Wisconsin, formed a union. These workers thus joined tens of thousands of mass production workers who surged into unions for the first time, in the wake of the National Industrial Recovery Act (NIRA). Over the next decade and a half, they survived challenges from management, consolidated their strength, and entered into the mainstream of organized labor. They kept their union intact through a bitter contract dispute in 1938 and 1939; during World War II, their ranks swelled and their production lines hummed incessantly as they provided critical supplies of electrical goods for the Signal Corps. Although sharply divided as to the scope, purposes, and style of trade unionism appropriate to their particular situation, the workers came quickly to view the union as an integral part of their working lives, even if it rarely assumed a major cultural role. The establishment, development, and tribulations of the union at Ray-O-Vac, while lacking the overt drama of the more spectacular labor events of the 1930s and 1940s, illustrate in microcosm basic themes in the recent history of American unionism.

The rise of the labor movement in the years of depression and war is one of the most significant developments in American recent history. Although there has been a tendency to discount or belittle the role of organized labor in American society—to dismiss it as a relic of a previous age or as merely a junior partner in the liberal corporate order—a good case can be made that the revitalization and expansion of the labor movement in the 1930s and 1940s was the most enduring progressive achievement of the New Deal era. Although their record on such issues as

1

foreign policy, civil rights, environmental concerns, and internal democracy is mixed and often wide of the targets that liberals and intellectuals have established, the unions remain the most vigorous and cohesive force in the country speaking with any effectiveness for broad masses of people. If to the general public the labor movement is barely observable at all, and if even among educated people there is little awareness of its structure, problems, or achievements, organized labor is nonetheless the leading advocate for economic and social policies in behalf of lower income groups. If organized labor is indeed an integral part of the corporate system, it is also that system's most persistent and effective critic.[1]

Much of the current lack of interest in and misunderstanding of American trade unionism stems from a distorted view of its history. Looming behind the prevalent images of palatial union headquarters, rampant corruption, and complacent labor bureaucrats is the specter of labor's heroic past. The vision of what labor ought to be is very much conditioned by a perception of what it once was. There is a tendency to contrast today's prosaic lobbying and nuts-and-bolts bargaining with the dramatic organizing drives and sitdown strikes of the 1930s; to contrast the flat, gravelly voice of George Meany with the stentorian tones of John L. Lewis, calling his miners and steelworkers to battle as he heaped scorn upon errant politicians, arrogant corporate owners, and fainthearted craft unionists; to contrast the jaunty, militant songs of Woody Guthrie and the Almanac Singers,[2] redolent of class conflict and filled with visions of a new day, with—what? The lonely plaints of Johnny Cash or Dave Dudley? And although the liberal public can occasionally arouse itself over the plight of visibly oppressed farm workers or garbage strikers, most workers who today walk a picket line do so most unheroically in a form of ritualized combat, risking neither life nor limb nor mortgage payment. Both leaders and rank and file alike seem to have come a long way from the coal mines of Harlan County, the bloody fields of South Chicago, and the grim factories of Flint.[3]

Although this contrast between current complacency and erstwhile vigor has elements of legitimacy, it is overdrawn. It rests upon grossly distorted impressions of the heroic 1930s, to say nothing of erroneous views of the present realities of trade unions and the working classes. It sees in the sporadic militancy of the past a coherent crusading radicalism, while it ignores much of today's laborite progressivism. It overlooks the antiunionism and apathy of many workers in the 1930s and the strength of old-fashioned individualism that persisted throughout the Depression. By focusing on a handful of spectacular events and dramatic confrontations of the 1930s, the currently fashionable view draws a sharp contrast between a glorious past and a mundane present. This oversimplified and distorted vision of the 1930s not only does violence to the past itself, it gets in the way of thinking about the present.

Without detracting from the courage and commitment displayed by the men and women who formed the modern American labor movement in the 1930s, it will be well to keep in mind some of the ambiguities and countertendencies of the period. For example, the organization of workers in the 1930s, despite unprecedented governmental endorsement and support and despite an unparalleled commitment of people, money, and energy by the labor movement, was sporadic and partial. It took four years before American workers were sufficiently aroused by the Depression to begin large-scale union building. At that, it required fortuitous federal legislation to trigger the first wave of unionism. A burst of energy and enthusiasm in the two years of the National Recovery Administration (NRA) was marred by large areas of apathy; even before the end of the NRA, wholesale defections had crippled many new unions. When the second wave of organization occurred in 1936 and 1937, it owed as much to centralized direction and generous financing as it did to grass-roots activism. Often CIO organizers encountered skepticism and indifference. Much of the successful AFL counterattack, which did so much in the late 1930s to expand membership figures, depended on cooperation with employers, pressure tactics, and top-down organization. Company unions flourished through the early 1930s, by no means always because of intimidation and manipulation. New locals formed in the 1930s were extremely volatile and highly susceptible to discouragement, personal influence, and company blandishments.[4]

Racial, religious, and ethnic animosities constantly impeded unionization in the 1930s and during World War II. In the steel industry, Anglo-American workers undercut the efforts of Eastern Europeans and Italians in behalf of the Steel Workers Organizing Committee. In the Middle West, Black Legionnaires, many of them working class, fought unionization. Even in the early 1940s, thousands of black auto workers identified closely with Henry Ford and resisted—sometimes heroically— UAW-CIO organizing efforts. Of course, racial and religious antagonisms posed constant stumbling blocks to unionization in the South, while seething rank-and-file militancy in war production plants during World War II frequently focused workers' resentment on female and minority workers.[5]

Moreover, millions of American workers remained impervious to the appeal of trade unionism, considering the unions too radical and too dangerous. Of those who joined, hundreds of thousands did so out of careful calculation of specific economic interests. The unions had to weigh and work through this instrumentalist view of unionism during even the most heroic days of the 1930s. It is sobering to realize that most of the activism of the 1930s had to do with basic, ordinary trade union demands, not with radical visions. The sitdown strikes, for example, were tactical weapons with which to secure union recognition, not a step toward worker control. Throughout the 1930s, time after time workers demonstrated that they sought union recognition, exclusive bargaining rights, seniority, and even the checkoff. Very little in either the organizing campaigns or the political activities of the unions in the 1930s was addressed to broad, social concerns, for the unions and their members were embroiled in a decade-long effort to establish the most elementary rights of organization and union security. Unions in the 1930s had neither the time nor the resources to devote to such class issues as medical care, income redistribution, taxation, education, and a whole series of social-economic reforms today regularly championed by the AFL-CIO and the independent unions.[6]

Although the recollections of activists sometimes make it seem otherwise, there was little leftist influence in the emerging labor movement. Most workers rejected all but the most conventional definitions of their political role. Despite the appeal of Socialists, Communists, and John L. Lewis himself, the American worker kept the picture of Franklin D. Roosevelt tacked to the wall. In a most unideological indulgence in the cult of personality, American workers frequently identified more thoroughly with the patrician from New York than they did with the organizations they had created and the union leaders they had chosen.

Indeed, the real story of what took place in the 1930s has

less to do with the emergence of a putatively radical, consistently militant force than it does with the collision of angry, confused, and frustrated workers with little acquaintance with the labor movement, with a trade union movement proud of its past, uncertain of its future, and profoundly ambivalent about its current course. It is this collision, with its impact on both workers and unions, that forms the enduring legacy of the 1930s and 1940s.

The drama was played out most decisively between 1933, when the National Industrial Recovery Act (NIRA) and its Section 7(a) were passed, and 1947, which marked the passage of the Labor-Management Relations Act. Before 1933, the labor movement was stagnant, seemingly moribund. By 1947, it had achieved massive numerical gains and had acquired the necessary political influence to preserve them. It was during this fourteen-year span that decisive numbers of relatively unskilled industrial workers joined labor unions. These years witnessed a vigorous internal debate between militant and moderate elements, not only as represented in the two great rival federations, but within scores of international unions and thousands of new local unions as well. It was this period in which labor legislation and crucial governmental administrative activities decisively altered the historic voluntarism and apolitical pretensions of the unions.

American workers faced these tensions and conflicts throughout the era of depression and war. The most notable confrontations pitted the rebel CIO against the established AFL; the punch with which John L. Lewis floored William Hutcheson in 1935 stands as a fitting image for labor's internal struggle. In many respects, however, fixation on the AFL-CIO conflict results in oversimplification. Internecine struggle also afflicted both federations. Factionalism within the United Auto Workers is legendary, and the showdown between Lewis and Philip Murray at the top of the CIO in the early 1940s reached deep into its ranks. As for the AFL, not all of those who supported industrial unionism and progressive social policies left the old federation. Throughout these years industrial unionists such as Patrick Gorman of the Meatcutters and John P. Burke of the Pulp, Sulphite Workers attacked bureaucratic tendencies within the federation and urged it to expand organizational efforts.

Federal labor unions (FLUs), local bodies directly affiliated with the AFL, reflected these tensions sharply and directly. By the late 1930s, the federation listed over 200,000 members of directly affiliated unions, a number that accounted for about 7 percent of its total membership and over 40 percent of its revenues. FLUs were by definition industrial in organizational structure. At the same time, they were weak within the federation's internal government, due to constitutional provisions that preserved the dominance of the large national unions at the AFL's annual convention and on the federation's Executive Council. They were in many cases temporary bodies, their primary purpose in the eyes of AFL officials being to hold workers until they could be doled out or taken over by the appropriate craft bodies. Still, many of the FLUs born in the 1930s had long lives. As industrial unions often in conflict locally with craft unions and as bodies without the kinds of historic and traditional connections with the hoary national unions that ran things in the AFL, the federal unions were anomalous and vaguely disconcerting to the federation's establishment.

Since the FLUs were so significant in channeling labor's response to the organizational opportunities of the 1930s, and since they represented such a large proportion of the production workers newly organized in that period, their story is important. Federal unionists responded in different ways to the stresses and tensions in the labor movement. Some, finding the AFL insufficiently interested in their problems or finding the presumed benefits of organization not readily attainable, quickly dropped out; the attrition rate among FLUs was high. Some FLUs did happily serve the purpose apparently envisaged for them in the AFL: once organized they either became absorbed into one of the national unions directly or had their members divided up into the appropriate craft organizations. And, of course, federal unions in autos, rubber, electrical appliances, and other industries formed the nuclei for the new national unions that, together with the industrial unionists already in the AFL, constituted the heart of the CIO.

Some newly organized workers, however, did none of these things but rather remained in directly affiliated bodies, seeking to find ways in which they could achieve local autonomy and broaden the influence of the federal unions within the federation while enjoying AFL service and support. Many of the conflicts observable on the national scene in the struggle between the AFL and CIO, between bureaucrats and militants, between voluntarists and politicals, were fought out on the grass-roots level, both between federal unionists and the AFL officialdom and among the federal unionists themselves.

Following is an account of the establishment and early history of one federal labor union. It focuses on the period of the Depression and World War II, the years during which the union was formed and underwent some of its most difficult trials. It seeks to grasp something of the unique reality of these particular workers' lives and activities, while at the same time putting them into the broader context of the general labor history of this period.

The union examined—Federal Labor Union 19587, AFL, Madison, Wisconsin—did not play a significant role in the major confrontations of the 1930s. Its members staged no historic strikes, nor did they participate in the storied industrial battles of the decade. To students of labor history, such places as Aliquippa, Youngstown, Akron, Flint, Toledo, and Gastonia evoke industrial conflict and working-class heroism. Madison, although the home of a university noted for its labor scholarship, would conjure up no such dramatic images.

Yet the marvelously preserved records of FLU 19587 are of more than antiquarian interest. The workers at the Ray-O-Vac Battery plant in Madison were among the tens of thousands who seized the opportunity afforded by the NIRA to form their first union. As semiskilled industrial workers, they encountered at firsthand the ambivalences and contradictions of the AFL as it responded to new organizational opportunities. As members of one of the thousands of federal labor unions formed at this time, the battery makers sought constantly to find ways to maximize their influence in the labor movement, struggling against the constraints that the AFL imposed on its directly affiliated unions. A child of the turbulent 1930s, 19587 fought bitterly with management, as both sides struggled to grasp the meaning of the new system of labor relations that emerged in that decade. The union underwent sharp internal controversies between militants and moderates; its internal history reveals much about the character and impact of the elusive but central phenomenon of the 1930s, rank-and-file militancy. The union and its members rose to meet the challenges of wartime production while at the same time preserving their union amid the unique pressures of industrial relations during World War II. Finally, 19587 emerged from the war troubled by the same questions that confronted the labor movement throughout the country. Its members had to prove anew that they could maintain an organization in the face of severe antilabor pressures. They had to decide again the virtues and appropriateness of vigorous militancy as against a stance of moderation and cooperation. They had to test whether the union they had created and nurtured could survive in the troubled postwar atmosphere.

Thus, although 19587 did not participate in the dramatic confrontations of the 1930s and 1940s, it did experience all of the major influences that shaped American labor history during these years. Moreover, its officers and members were articulate, well informed, and deeply involved in the labor movement. Readers of the following pages will learn something about the process of local union formation and about the impact of federal legislation and administrative procedures on unionization, both in the 1930s and during World War II. They will be able to observe some of the tensions between militancy and apathy that affected local unions and the labor movement as a whole. They will be able to follow from a grass-roots perspective the role of the AFL, the course of collective bargaining, and other significant topics. FLU 19587's extensive records, together with the vivid recollections of some of its most active members, perhaps compensate for the local's lack of glamour and fame. They may even help to redress the balance of labor history by revealing something of the drama and significance in the activities of "ordinary" people who lived through this extraordinary epoch.

II.
Before the Union

Before the establishment of Federal Labor Union 19587 in May 1934, the Ray-O-Vac Battery company had had little contact with trade unionism. Founded and incorporated in 1906, it eventually located in Madison more because of chance and the general attractiveness of the area than for any economic reason. Some local businessmen, led by J. B. Ramsay, grew interested in the dry cell battery as an opportunity for investment. Ramsay saw in the emerging automobile and mechanized farm implement industries a natural market for such batteries and persuaded several local merchants and lawyers, who came to constitute the company's early board of directors, to invest in the business and to move it from Chicago, where it had originated, to Madison. Originally named French Battery and Carbon Company, the new concern weathered several difficult years before certain technical problems were solved through the efforts of Professor Charles E. Burgess, head of the University of Wisconsin's Department of Chemical Engineering. Employment grew from a handful of operatives in the very early days to 275 in 1920, 500 in 1930, and more than 800 in 1940. The company's name was changed to Ray-O-Vac in 1934. During World War II Ray-O-Vac became a major producer of batteries for the Signal Corps, employing nearly 2,000 workers in Madison. Since then decentralization of the company's operations and automation have cut the labor force drastically.

During most of its first fifty years, the company was based in Madison and locally owned. By the 1930s, it had established facilities in such places as Fond du Lac and Wonewoc, Wisconsin; Clinton, Massachusetts; and Lancaster, Ohio; but its major era of expansion, both geographical and in terms of capitalization and resulting ownership, was after World War II.[1]

The company's labor force also was largely homegrown. Although in the heartland of the Middle West's industrial region, Madison itself is a city dominated by state government employment, the University of Wisconsin, and other white-collar activity. Throughout most of the twentieth century, the city's population closely reflected the Yankee and Old Immigration character of the surrounding countryside, with high percentages of people of English, Scandinavian, and German backgrounds. Moreover, relatively few of its inhabitants were first- or second-generation immigrants, in sharp contrast to the ethnic patterns of such nearby industrial cities as Rockford, Illinois, and Milwaukee, Kenosha, and Racine, Wisconsin.

Industry in Madison, never a major industrial center, was (and is) concentrated on the east side of the city, where the largest enterprises—Gisholt Machinery, Oscar Mayer, Ohio Chemical, and Ray-O-Vac—were based. The Capitol Square, situated astride a narrow neck of land separating Lakes Monona and Mendota, divides industrial eastern Madison from the academic and residential western part of the city. Most of the city's industrial workers resided east of the capital, commonly in detached single-family dwellings. Although working-class Madison did have its elements of distinctive cultural life, which by the 1930s focused primarily on the east side's taverns, bowling alleys, and union halls, there were no discernible ethnic ghettos or large tracts of slum housing.[2]

The presence of the university and other government agencies in Madison both hindered and encouraged the city's labor movement. On the one hand, academic and civil service employment characterized the labor force, making an industrial labor movement something of an anomaly.[3] In a city where a relatively small proportion of the labor force was blue collar, the values and aspirations of the salaried white-collar element dominated. In more practical terms, Madison's blue-collar workers found a sharp housing and income division in the community, as expensive residential construction west of the square and university largely excluded factory hands. Ray-O-Vac workers in the 1930s, for example, were keenly aware of the housing inadequacies of working-class Madison, and felt that local builders concentrated on the more lucrative university and government residential market on the west side. One of 19587's earliest and most frequently voiced political stands was support for federal housing legislation.[4]

But the presence of the university, together with the general progressive political tradition of Wisconsin, had its advantages for working-class Madisonians. The university may have been physically remote from the factories, but the faculty's liberal orientation created an atmosphere that often supported trade unionism. Professors from the university frequently addressed local union meetings, and a number of 19587's members attended the Extension Division's School for Workers in Industry at the university. Ray-O-Vac's unionists made direct use of university people in collective bargaining matters, and the state AFL leadership enjoyed cordial and productive associations with members of the economics faculty and with experts in the Extension Division and the Law School. By the 1930s the Department of Economics, through the trailblazing work of Richard T. Ely, John R. Commons, Selig Perlman, and other scholars, had established the university as one of the nation's leading centers of labor history and labor studies. While the activities of Perlman's seminar did not directly affect the Ray-O-Vac production line, the sympathetic labor scholarship at the university did help to narrow the gap between workbench and classroom.[5]

If the presence of the university made Madison an unusual environment for industrial workers, the circumstances of the battery trade were also unique. Although French Battery was locally owned and operated, it produced primarily for a national market. Moreover, it was dependent for raw materials and semifinished components upon suppliers around the country and even overseas. Thus, from the start, French Battery was closely tied to the local community both through formal ownership and through custom and background; at the same time it was deeply involved in national and international markets, in regard both to sales and to acquisition of raw materials. There was, as company officials frequently pointed out to dissident workers in the 1930s, no intrinsic reason for Ray-O-Vac's location in Madison and hence no reason why the company could not pull up stakes if its employees became unreasonable.[6]

The early labor policies of the company remain obscure. We do not know if French Battery employees participated in the spasm of post–World War I strikes that affected other plants in Madison. We have no record of attempts before 1934 of employees to organize bona fide trade unions, although one veteran Ray-O-Vac employee recalls that in the late 1920s the threat of an AFL union induced another Madison battery concern to move operations to Dubuque, Iowa.[7] Fortunately, however, we can infer some of the policies and attitudes toward employees that French Battery's managers embraced from the pages of the employees' association newspaper.

In the post–World War I atmosphere, many large corporations turned toward various schemes of employee representation, welfare work, and rationalized personnel policies as a means of securing the loyalty of their employees and inhibiting the growth of labor unions. These plans ranged from simple sponsorship of recreational activities or exhortative pleas for loyalty and productivity to rather elaborate programs of employee representation through shop councils or even industrial assemblies. By the late 1920s, one expert counted more than four million American workers enrolled in some form of employee welfare activity. To many observers, including some normally sympathetic to the goals of the labor movement, welfare capitalism seemed a permanent feature of the American industrial scene.[8]

Most of these programs sprang up relatively late in the 1920s, and most were installed in the larger corporations. Thus, French Battery and Carbon Company was innovative in its efforts to provide its 250 or so employees with the blessings of harmonious organization under company auspices. In July 1919 the French Battery and Carbon Company Employees' Association was born, along with its newspaper, the *French Flasher*. Though it consistently disclaimed editorial control by the company, the publication functioned as a company newsletter. Similarly, although the association itself was portrayed as a genuinely democratic expression of all employees, management and office personnel dominated it. The employees' association remained in existence through the 1950s, although after the coming of the union it devoted its attentions to running the factory canteen and conducting charitable drives. The newspaper, which in the 1920s had pretensions to serving as the real voice of company employees, became by the 1950s (and probably much earlier) merely a company organ.

Whatever the subsequent career of the association and the newsletter, in the 1920s it seems to have represented a real effort on the part of the company to provide a form of cohesive association for the employees. Apparently the brainchild of J. B. Ramsay, president of the company from 1906 to 1934, the association proclaimed that its initial purpose was "to bring all of us together in a closer relationship."[9] Throughout the 1920s, the association sought to foster the idea of the company as an institution that transcended profit and loss, wages and hours. An editorial in the first newsletter noted approvingly that employees habitually referred to the plant as "our factory." The newsletter sought to project Ramsay as both more and less than a company president. On the one hand, he was portrayed as unusually farsighted and fair-minded, while on the other he was, in a sense, merely another employee engaged in the common work.[10]

The association and the newspaper constantly exhorted employees to improve themselves and to avoid bad habits. They were urged to attend YMCA classes, to worship at the churches of their choice, and to contribute to worthy community charities. Above all, they were encouraged to identify directly, both economically and psychologically, with the company and its fortunes. The November 1919 issue quoted Elbert Hubbard on the dangers of knocking one's employer, who was, after all, one's benefactor. A subsequent issue warned against the dangers of brooding about one's wages. The worker, advised the newspaper, should not worry about what the company was doing for him or for her but rather, "What am I doing for my company?"[11]

A major instrument for creating positive feelings about the company was its sponsorship of picnics, athletic events, and social affairs. The newspaper devoted much of its space to detailing the activities of the French Battery baseball squad, which compiled an enviable record in the 1920s. Bowling and basketball also received prominent attention. The association itself met quarterly, with community sings, dances, and general camaraderie easily overshadowing its few business functions. For the female employees, there was the Ray-O-Lite Club, a group of young women who met at the YMCA for sewing sessions and uplifting conversation and speeches. The company sponsored lunchtime sing-alongs led by a university professor. Holidays were occasions for companywide parties, replete with songs, dancing, hijinks, and speeches from company executives. At the 1919 Christmas party, the association presented Mr. Ramsay with a toilet set for traveling.

In addition to sponsoring the association, the newspaper, athletic activities, and songfests, the company did venture cautiously into the unfamiliar terrain of welfare capitalism. In a move unusual for smaller companies in the 1920s, French Battery created a separate Personnel Department to recruit and train workers. Its director urged the employees to view him as a friend and counselor. He was the link between employee and management, of course, but he was also someone to whom employees could turn to share their hopes and dreams and problems. The Personnel Department had a subsection dealing with "Social Betterment—First Aid." What the first phrase entailed is not clear, but in implementing the latter function, the company employed a plant nurse. In addition to administering first aid, she wrote a monthly column entitled "Health Hints."[12]

Although the newsletter and employee association both proclaimed their freedom from management control, both were in fact adjuncts of the plant administration. Apparently few production workers attended association functions, at least if the frequent scoldings of the newspaper about poor turnouts are any indication. And, although both the association and the newspaper sought to convey the impression that they were organs of the entire work force, virtually all of the reporters and association activists were drawn from management or from the office staff. Still, if these organs offer little insight into the daily lives or activities of production workers, they do reveal much about the expectations and aspirations of management vis-à-vis the workers. Probably more indicative of these goals or hopes than any single function of the association is the general tone of the newspaper. Throughout its pages, workers are pictured as happy, contented participants in a common enterprise. The columns are filled with little jokes and gossipy tidbits about members of the work force. Glee clubs, ball teams, and bowling squads invariably carried some company designation, often some sort of play on words. Although there was an occasional warning against the dangers of radical propaganda, the main effort of the newsletter was to ingratiate the employees, to encourage them to identify with the goals and corporate image of the company. Perhaps dimly aware of the alienating character of production work, perhaps fearful of labor unionism, perhaps genuinely desirous of implementing its paternalistic version of employee welfare, French Battery and Carbon Company sought to assure the loyalty and good cheer of its operatives. "Have you ever noticed how peacefully our factory runs?" asked one executive in his column. "The carbon grinders 'grind' all day and the Tampers 'tamp' away. Then," he continued, "you go over to the flashlight side and see Elmer's bunch 'rolling' along and the cans 'seam' so easy."[13]

It is doubtful that many production workers shared this halcyon vision of the company's operations. By the late 1920s, Madison's workers felt French Battery took advantage of the lack of industrial employment in the city to hold to a very modest wage structure. Workers complained about the seasonal nature of employment,* flagrant favoritism in work assignments, lack of seniority safeguards, split shifts, and the unwillingness of management to compensate employees for time spent awaiting assignments after being called in to work. Although the impact of the early years of the Depression proved less severe for French Battery than for many other manufacturing concerns, there was certainly no improvement in wage rates or working conditions during those difficult years.[14]

---

*Ray-O-Vac stockpiled batteries in the winter when labor was more readily available. During this time of year, farmers and other outdoor workers sought factory employment.

III.
Starting the Union

Despite their dissatisfaction with the company, French Battery workers in the 1920s had displayed little interest in trade unionism. The weakness and lassitude of the labor movement in that decade discouraged even ardent laborites around the country. In addition, most Madison workers had roots directly in the countryside of the Midwest. Few battery workers had had earlier contact with unions, nor was there a substantial element in the plant with immigrant radical background. In some industries that unionized suddenly in the 1930s, men and women with family histories in the mine workers or in the Socialist party led the way, but French Battery workers reflected Wisconsin's sturdy progressivism.

As it turned out, the absence of a laborite background made little difference, for the battery workers brought important strengths to their efforts to create a union. They were a literate and articulate group, perhaps reflecting the value that Wisconsinites attached to education. Moreover, while few had grown up in a trade union environment, some were products of the La Follette progressive political tradition; if their social milieu had not included unions, their political backgrounds were squarely in the dissenting, progressive tradition. Ray-O-Vac employees were usually able to find energetic spokesmen and spokeswomen for their common grievances, for their individualism was one of protest and political activism, not simply a negative agrarian privatism.[1]

The birth of the union at Ray-O-Vac was intimately bound up with the emergence of mass unionism in Wisconsin. Following the passage of the National Industrial Recovery Act in June 1933, Henry Ohl, Jr., and J. J. Handley, president and secretary-treasurer respectively of the Wisconsin State Federation of Labor (WSFL), eagerly seized upon Section 7(a) to spur organization. Throughout the summer and fall of 1933, organizing campaigns achieved immediate success in laborite

Milwaukee, while around the state, even in cities previously immune to the union appeal, workers surged into the unions. "Labor chieftains," observed one state newspaper, "regard the current activity as the greatest single advance in [the state's] union history."[2]

Nor was the WSFL particularly concerned with traditional methods of organization or jurisdictional boundaries. In Kenosha, Racine, Milwaukee, Manitowoc, Two Rivers, Janesville, and other cities in the state's industrial belt there toiled tens of thousands of workers in metal fabrication, farm implements, autos and auto parts, furniture, aluminum, and other mass production industries, largely ignored by the crafts, but now ripe for unionism. The state federation and its organizers actively recruited these unskilled and semiskilled workers. Ohl addressed mass meetings in several cities and, in the absence of organizers from national unions, urged workers to take out federal charters directly from the AFL. At times, in a spirit reminiscent of the old mixed assemblies of the Knights of Labor and the One Big Union dream of the Wobblies, workers signed up helter-skelter, regardless of place of employment, under a common federal charter. Thus, from the beginning of the resurgence of organized labor in Wisconsin, federal labor unions, though often regarded as anomalous appendages or temporary holding bodies elsewhere, received the enthusiastic support of the state's labor establishment and assumed a significant role in the experience of the state's workers.[3]

It was natural, then, that as Ray-O-Vac's workers caught the union fever, they would apply for a federal charter. Apparently no single dramatic event triggered the establishment of the union. Veterans of its early days recall simply that in 1933 and 1934, in view of general difficulties with the company and because of a desire to improve their lot, a group of workers became interested in trade unionism. The decision to form a union seemed logical and appropriate, an extension rather than a negation of their stiff-backed individualism. William McCutchin, who had worked in the toolroom since 1923, was the leading spirit, visiting workers after hours and defying his supervisors' warnings to stop stirring up trouble. In May 1934, "a few of us decided we should organize a Union," recorded one of the founders. "We met at the Labor Temple [one] evening and signed up for a charter with the A.F. of L." It was that simple.[4]

Although many of the federal unions established in the wake of the NIRA quickly collapsed, 19587 survived an early challenge from management and firmly established itself among the employees. David Saposs, a leading academic authority on industrial unionism, declared in 1934 that the fate of these newly formed FLUs would be "the crucial test of the ability of American unions to organize the basic industries and to exist as a vital movement." The attrition rate among FLUs was high between 1933 and 1935, however, as fledgling organizations succumbed to employers' coercion and blandishments, found the government weak in its support of the alleged guarantees of Section 7(a), or found the established labor movement unresponsive, contemptuous, and suspicious. The union at Ray-O-Vac surmounted these obstacles and throughout the 1930s maintained a relatively high level of organization.[5]

Ray-O-Vac employees supported the union loyally during its crucial formative years. An AFL report for 1936 put the average monthly membership since the union's inception at 260, an impressive figure given the seasonal nature of the battery trade and the chronic difficulties that many new unions encountered in collecting dues. Although local leaders frequently complained of poor attendance at meetings and erratic dues payment, the minute books usually recorded over a hundred members present at meetings throughout the 1930s, suggesting that the officers' complaints owed more to their own fervor and expectations than to any unusual failings on the part of the membership. Of course, both membership and attendance increased during controversies with management, and in general the union was able to retain the active interest of at least some among the newly aroused. Because there was no automatic dues checkoff, the union had to rely on constant contact with the membership and the workers' sustained and active support to maintain itself in the 1930s. By 1937, union officials claimed 80 percent organization, a figure that seems too high as an indication of regular dues-paying support, although it is clear that by this time the union was accepted by most employees. Certainly, in contrast with many local unions formed in the ebullient days of 1933 and 1934, Federal Labor Union 19587 took root among the workers rapidly and firmly. In all, given the low-keyed and even cautious nature of the work force, which included many older women particularly fearful of work stoppages and susceptible to company threats to move operations elsewhere, the degree of attachment to the union is impressive.[6]

Of course, the willingness of Ray-O-Vac workers to embrace and support the union depended largely on its effectiveness in conducting collective bargaining. The union's struggle to pry concessions from a reluctant management, to improve working conditions and rates of pay, and to reduce some of the arbitrariness and insecurity characteristic of employment in the Madison factory posed the basic test of its ability to survive and grow. Throughout the 1930s, relations between 19587 and Ray-O-Vac veered sharply between easy accommodation and rancorous dispute. The pattern was not one of increasing maturity and stability through collective bargaining, but neither was it one of intransigent mutual antagonism. Periodically, the company executives behaved in such a way as to convince many workers of the company's determination to weaken or even break the union. This was not a systematic policy, however, and the company gradually displayed a willingness to bargain, at least in a de facto way, with union representatives. In 1937, the company signed a union shop agreement with 19587, but only after a particularly bitter dispute the previous year. The signing of this agreement did not signal harmony, however, for in November 1938 a union-management dispute led to a shutdown, which lasted into February 1939. In short, while labor-management relations at Ray-O-Vac lacked some of the drama of the Flint sit-down and the Little Steel strike, neither did they settle quickly into benign patterns of narrow, ritualized negotiations presumably common to mature industrial relations.

Trade unionism was as new to Ray-O-Vac's management as it was to the workers. The company president, W. W. Cargill, viewed the labor provisions of the NIRA suspiciously. Unschooled in the nature and functions of labor unions, he had to call on his father-in-law, a veteran of one of the railroad brotherhoods, to educate him.[7] At first the company limited its relationship with the union to the letter of the law, and not always even that. Although they had no carefully thought-out antilabor program, company executives apparently hoped that the union fever would die out and that Ray-O-Vac could soon return to its customary methods of employee relations.

Ray-O-Vac had no overt union-breakers on its staff, but the company did harass the union in a sporadic and haphazard way. For example, it failed to post the labor provisions of the code of fair competition for the battery industry, as required by the

NRA for firms such as Ray-O-Vac that sought the advantages of doing business under the code. Company officials closely questioned early union supporters about their activities and in May 1934 laid off five of them, including William McCutchin, the leader in the organizing campaign, immediately after the local's initial meeting. This move nearly precipitated a work stoppage. Sol Reist, the Madison Federation of Labor organizer who was advising the new local, reported that a strike vote would be taken "as the men are desperate." With a nervous eye focused on the explosive middle western labor milieu of 1934, he added darkly that he feared "another Toledo affair in Madison." The aggrieved unionists eventually appealed to the Chicago Regional Labor Board, which functioned as the regional office of the National Labor Board, and won reinstatement. Even so, the company resisted the board's intrusion into its affairs, consistently denied any connection between the layoff of the workers and their participation in union affairs, and delayed returning them to work.[8] Thus, despite this early victory, union representatives realized that the company could easily, within the permissive boundaries of existing legislation, which provided little more than rhetorical endorsement of workers' rights, utilize delay and obfuscation to avoid real collective bargaining.

Neither the battery industry in general nor Ray-O-Vac in particular enjoyed a reputation among workers for generous treatment of employees or pleasant working conditions. Many of the operations in manufacturing dry cell batteries involved the handling of carbon, asphalt, and harsh chemicals. Most jobs required little skill or initiative but called for careful visual and tactile attention, thus combining routinization with tension. Low wages characterized the industry, partly because of the semi-skilled nature of the work and partly because battery factories, which were usually in rural and quasi-rural areas, were able to tap reservoirs of seasonal farm workers and females. Although Eveready had a major plant in Cleveland, much of the country's battery production took place in Lancaster, Ohio; Freeport, Illinois; Dubuque and Sioux City, Iowa; Williamsport, Pennsylvania; Paducah, Kentucky; and Wausau, Fond du Lac, Wonewoc, and Madison, Wisconsin. Labor organizers and other unionists in Wisconsin viewed workers in the battery trade as unfortunate and disadvantaged, sympathizing with Ray-O-Vac's employees especially because the company, although its wages compared favorably with those paid by competitors, was widely regarded as stingy, stubborn, and eccentric. Its contracts, declared one veteran federal unionist and AFL organizer, were often "weird," containing quirky clauses dealing with vacations, seniority, and other matters. Once the company's leadership grew accustomed to the notion that the union was there to stay, they were willing enough to grant the union shop, but they bargained hard for every nickel and showed little desire to join the union in seeking to change the battery trade's reputation for backwardness in labor relations and employee compensation.[9]

The union bargained with management through a grievance committee elected by the membership. The local called for and received help from the AFL Regional Office and from Wisconsin State Federation of Labor organizers operating out of Milwaukee. The AFL representatives participated actively in the bargaining process and at times seem to have been the primary spokesmen for the union, although aggressive local leaders frequently followed their own counsel and opposed AFL recommendations. When the local committee reached an agreement with Ray-O-Vac, it submitted and explained its terms to the membership, which had the final voice. In addition, the negotiating team often came before the membership during negotiations to sample opinions about particular features of the contract before the agreement was written.

Union veterans regard Ray-O-Vac as having been a tough and difficult bargainer. Moderates in the union sympathized with the company's disadvantageous competitive position in the battery industry and were extremely sensitive to the company's threats to move operations out of Madison if the union pressed unreasonable demands. The presence of large numbers of "second income" female employees and the lack of alternative industrial employment in Madison reinforced the tendency toward a modest negotiating stance on the part of the union. On the other hand, 19587 had its share of militants who viewed Ray-O-Vac's threats as bluffs and who felt that the company was in a far better position to upgrade its wage scale than its officials admitted. Despite the tendencies toward moderation, the members of 19587 were entirely willing to reject settlements and to back negotiating demands with strike votes. Whatever their internal disagreements, the battery workers showed militancy and solidarity whenever the company seemed to be attacking the union. Between 1934 and 1948, the union passed strike votes on at least four occasions. Although 19587's members did not actually walk a picket line during this period, on more than one occasion they chose their picket captains and had their signs printed before last-minute settlements. Over the years, Ray-O-Vac and Federal Labor Union 19587 were regular customers of the National Labor Relations Board, the War Labor Board, and the United States Conciliation Service.[10]

Spurts of tension and reconciliation characterized the first several years of the relationship between the company and the union. In August 1934, just three months after the company officials responded to the initial organization of 19587 by laying off the activists, the union issued an open letter to Ray-O-Vac's customers, declaring its moderate intentions and assuring the business world that relations between labor and management were stable and harmonious. In December, the membership "gave the Ray-O-Vac Co. a rising vote of thanks" for the year-end bonus and expressed the hope that labor-management relations in the new year would be as harmonious as those in 1934.[11]

Nevertheless, Ray-O-Vac was reluctant to enter into a contractual relationship with the union. Local 19587's secretary reported in August 1935, "Our Employer has never refused to bargain with us," but the vague and elaborate series of conferences that company and union officials held throughout the spring and summer of 1935 fell far short of bona fide collective bargaining. For its part, the company demurred at the strict application of seniority in making seasonal work force adjustments. Moreover, company officials felt uncomfortable about the union's reliance on Ed Hall, a militant Wisconsin auto worker and at the time a volunteer AFL organizer, for negotiating advice. Unionists criticized the company for the slowness with which it had implemented earlier agreements and for its generally dilatory and confusing response to the union's request for information and workplace adjustments. Unionists feared that the company hoped to erode rank-and-file support through a policy of delay and petty confusion. In view of the protracted nature of the negotiations and the company's unwillingness to enter into a specific collective bargaining contract, the union voted in April 1935 to withdraw its letter of assurance of uninterrupted production, earlier sent to major Ray-O-Vac customers. On August 12, after a lengthy period of ill-defined quasi-negotiations concerning wage rates, union recognition, grievance procedures, and other matters, the membership rejected a vague company offer of an informal working agreement. Eventually, at the suggestion of Hall, the union requested the efforts of a conciliator from the United States Conciliation Service (USCS).[12]

Robert Mythen of the USCS arrived in Madison on September 18. He reported that the union membership had rejected another vague Ray-O-Vac proposal. In addition, he found that Cargill refused to compromise and stood adamantly against entering into a collective bargaining arrangement with the union. After considerable consultation with both sides, Mythen secured an agreement. On October 1, the union membership voted approval of a document that granted concessions in such matters as seniority and grievances and specified that the company would bargain concerning wages, hours, and conditions of employment with a three-person committee representing unionized production workers. The document went on to assure nonunion employees that they could approach the management individually or through their own, separately chosen representatives. These provisions suggested a kind of de facto acceptance by the company of the fact of widespread union membership, but at the same time they revealed that Ray-O-Vac was reluctant to award 19587 official recognition.[13]

Mythen described this document as a collective bargaining agreement, but it was one only in the loosest sense. By withholding recognition and encouraging employees to deal with management on an individual basis, the company may have hoped that the union would lose influence. Certainly, the 1935 document imposed heavy restrictions, backed up by harsh penalties, against the solicitation of union membership or the discussion of union business on company premises. Although there is no evidence that Ray-O-Vac contemplated the creation of a company union, a device to which many other employers resorted in the 1930s in their efforts to undermine trade unionism, the terms of the 1935 agreement convinced many of the unionists of the company's hostility.

Then in the spring of 1936 a quarrel erupted resulting in Ray-O-Vac's dismissal of two union leaders. This action deepened unionists' suspicion and resentment. On one level the quarrel revealed the inexperience of both the company and the union. Both were unfamiliar with the practice of industrial relations and displayed impatience and lack of wisdom in the critical area of grievance handling. On another level, however, the month-long dispute represented a major challenge to the union and a significant effort on the part of the company to test 19587 and its membership. The difficulties that occurred, the negotiations that followed, and the resulting settlement were crucial events in 19587's struggle to survive.

The 1935 document allowed workers in production departments to choose stewards, who were to have direct access to the Ray-O-Vac Personnel Department in grievance matters. The document also assumed that the three men—William McCutchin, William Skaar, and Max Onsager—named to conduct collective bargaining with the company were to serve as a kind of overall grievance committee as well, at least insofar as union members were concerned. Although the 1935 document did not specify exclusive union responsibility for grievance handling, everyone in the plant knew that McCutchin, Skaar, and Onsager were prominent members of 19587 and that McCutchin and Skaar were, respectively, president and vice-president of the local.

The dispute began on April 7 when a foreman discharged Andy Christianson, a union production worker, for allegedly refusing to obey orders. The controversy concerned the foreman's demand that Christianson work a split shift, a practice common at Ray-O-Vac but one resented strongly by production workers. According to company officials, Christianson had been given a legitimate assignment in the normal way. He had consulted with Skaar and McCutchin as to whether he was obliged to accept the assignment. Without advising Christianson of the regular grievance procedures, the two union officials urged him to disobey his foreman's orders. Upon following this recommendation, Christianson was fired.

Christianson's dismissal created dismay among unionists, but open opposition erupted shortly after when Ray-O-Vac announced the firing of both McCutchin and Skaar. The company charged the two union leaders with arbitrary interference with its prerogatives and with sabotaging its authority. Cargill denied that his action signaled an attack on the union, declaring that it was in reality the two union leaders who had undermined the spirit of the 1935 agreement by their gratuitous encouragement of Christianson's insubordination. No union business was involved, the president argued; the matter was closed. He would gladly meet with a reconstituted grievance committee (Skaar and McCutchin being ineligible since they were no longer in the employ of Ray-O-Vac), but he blankly refused to reinstate any of the three men or to agree to arbitration of the dispute.[14]

Throughout the controversy, company officials acted imperiously. Unionists responded with truculence and resentment. Shortly after the original incident took place, Cargill called each of the three principals separately into his office for interviews. He chided Christianson, an inarticulate production worker, and elicited from him the implication that Skaar and McCutchin had advised him to defy his foreman. McCutchin, then the union president, proved somewhat more obdurate. He insisted that his advice to Christianson was in the way of an informal comment and in no way violated the company's prerogatives or the rudimentary grievance procedures established in 1935. He bridled at what he considered "cross examination" by Cargill. In the end, however, he succumbed to the persistent interrogation and gave verbal agreement to Cargill's carefully phrased interpretation of events.

With Skaar, Cargill met a dead end. The union vice-president challenged the legitimacy of the entire proceedings, arguing that the whole matter was union business and had to come before the Grievance Committee. He refused to discuss the situation on an individual basis. Realizing that Cargill could easily find discrepancies between statements made by the three unionists in the separate interviews, Skaar asked what McCutchin had said, whereupon Cargill snapped, "I'm asking *you* questions." Continuously rebuffing Cargill's demand that he speak as an individual, Skaar accused the official of trying to destroy the union. He eventually won the right to confer with McCutchin and Onsager before answering further questions. After a brief consultation among the three union leaders, Skaar returned to Cargill's office to inform him that they would answer no more questions and would wire the AFL and federal authorities for advice and conciliation help.[15]

Whether or not Ray-O-Vac consciously sought to destroy the union's influence through these dismissals, its officials could hardly have been surprised when the battery workers interpreted the firings as an assault on 19587. Skaar was convinced that the company was "taking picks on the union" through him. David Sigman, the AFL representative sent to Madison by William Green to investigate, agreed. He acknowledged the company's assertion that it was dealing with Skaar and

McCutchin only "as individuals," but he was convinced that Ray-O-Vac's action was "an attempt to break the labor organization by discharging its most active and responsible members." On April 13, the members of Federal Labor Union 19587 voted overwhelmingly to authorize a work stoppage against the company as a means of securing reinstatement of their leaders. The next night they listened as Sigman "gave advice and answered questions of what to do in case of a strike."[16]

To the relief of almost everyone, no strike occurred. On May 1, Sigman endorsed the local's request for AFL strike sanction, declaring to Green that it was "necessary to the welfare of organized labor that the men discharged be re-instated." Green approved his recommendation, but both AFL officials hoped for a prestrike settlement. Soon after taking its strike vote on April 13, the union had sought the aid of Region 12 of the National Labor Relations Board, headquartered in Milwaukee. Skaar appeared before the board, and Nathaniel Clark, director of Region 12, tried unsuccessfully to induce Ray-O-Vac to agree to arbitrate the dispute. Eventually, 19587 brought charges of unfair labor practices against the company, charging it with discrimination against union members, under the provisions of the National Labor Relations Act. Meanwhile, Sigman contacted Dean Lloyd K. Garrison of the University of Wisconsin Law School, a personal friend and former chairman of the NLRB, for informal help. In addition, the United States Conciliation Service entered the picture on May 4 with the arrival of Commissioner Robert Mythen.

With the union, backed by the AFL, determined to strike in support of McCutchin and Skaar, and the company immune to the combined blandishments of Clark, Garrison, and Mythen, a strike seemed certain. At the last minute, however, the company—likely at the suggestion of Mythen, who conferred continually with Cargill during the second week in May— offered a compromise. It would reinstate the three unionists after ninety days, provided they publicly acknowledge responsibility for the dispute and pledge to recognize the company's sole right to make work assignments. On May 14, at the urging of Sigman, Garrison, Clark, and Mythen, the membership unanimously accepted the proposal and agreed to compensate McCutchin, Skaar, and Christianson for their lost time.[17]

Despite the ungenerous terms of the settlement, it was a milestone in the union's development. Sigman noted that the battery workers had rallied enthusiastically to the union in the face of Ray-O-Vac's challenge and that it had, "since the controversy began, increased its membership."[18] Although it must have been distasteful for a strong-willed man such as Skaar to have signed a public statement accepting the company's interpretation of events, he used his free time to work on union affairs and to broaden contacts with battery workers elsewhere. While Ray-O-Vac had the satisfaction of wringing verbal concessions from the two union leaders, it had succeeded in enhancing rather than in discrediting their influence among their fellow workers. Upon reinstatement, Skaar returned to an active role in the union. While some of their cohorts may have resented the trouble and expense their actions caused, many more were heartened by the willingness of Skaar and McCutchin to stand up to the company. Had their dismissals stood uncontested, the union would have been crippled or destroyed. With the solidarity displayed by the membership and the eventual reinstatement of the two controversial men, it was strengthened.[19]

To Sigman, the lesson of the 1936 dispute was clear: both the union and the company had to face up to the realities of mature collective bargaining. The union had to be schooled in the handling of grievances and in the need for caution and tact in its approaches to the company. At the same time, he told Green, "I believe that some time in the near future it will have to be determined . . . whether or not the company intends . . . to come to [an] . . . understanding on working conditions, wages and hours through the form of a signed agreement."[20]

The 1936 controversy did indeed spur union and management into a more regular relationship. The May agreement, which led to the eventual reinstatement of Skaar, McCutchin, and Christianson, was followed in the fall by a signed contract governing wages, seniority, grievances, and working conditions. On March 4, 1937, the parties entered into a union shop agreement. Thus, beginning in 1936 annual negotiations provided a continuing contractual relationship between union and management, a relationship virtually unimaginable at Ray-O-Vac before 1934 but one that rapidly supplanted ties of personal loyalty, sentiment, or individual employment arrangements with the company in the minds of most workers.[21]

The establishment of the union and the achievement of signed contracts had a palpable impact on the working lives of Ray-O-Vac production employees. Late in 1939, Gerald Lochner, at various times union president and chairman of the Grievance Committee, discussed the first five years of the union on a statewide radio broadcast—"Glances from a Worker's World." Lochner described the work performed at Ray-O-Vac, tracing the manufacture of a dry cell battery from the grinding of the carbon in the mill room through the mixing, core tamping, ripening, testing, and final assembly operations. He commented briefly on some of the social functions and political concerns of the union. Mainly, however, he sought to convey to his listeners on the Wisconsin State Broadcasting network some sense of the day-to-day impact of the union on the lives of the 600 battery workers at Ray-O-Vac. Wage rates, he noted, had risen from 23 cents and 32 cents per hour for women and men respectively in 1933 to 37½ cents and 45 cents in 1939. He described the grievances that had festered before the establishment of the union, declaring that workers had feared to express complaints lest they be accused of dissidence and their jobs put in jeopardy. For Lochner, it was the establishment of a grievance committee, with the ability to give voice to workers' complaints, more than reductions in hours or wage increases, that was most important to the workers.[22]

Years later, another early activist, Evelyn Gotzion, recalled the start of her long involvement with the union in the late 1930s. At one point, the company instituted a new piece rate system, the operation of which mystified the workers. Some of the older women became frantic over their loss in income and their inability to keep pace with the new and complex formula. Gotzion seethed with anger over this disregard for hardworking people. After voicing her displeasure with this mistreatment, she found herself chosen departmental steward, despite her previous lack of interest in holding office. Once chosen, however, she shut down the line until the piece rates were explained and the most glaring inequities rectified. She recalls vividly the reaction of one older woman, a long-term employee, when a seniority system governing seasonal layoffs was negotiated by the union in 1937. For years this woman had felt sick with fear every spring, for it invariably appeared to her that the pretty girls who could joke and flirt with the foremen were kept on, while older women were laid off. To this woman, the freedom that the union represented was real and tangible, a matter as much of personal dignity as of economic security. It was in ways such as this that the union most directly entered into the lives of the battery workers.[23]

The battery workers' achievements were less spectacular than those of other American workers in the mid-1930s. Yet, they had shown courage and shrewdness in dealing with a recalcitrant employer. They had preserved and strengthened their union; despite later controversies, it would never again have its very existence challenged. A combination of militant leadership, rank-and-file steadfastness, and vigorous AFL support had proven effective. If 19587's achievement did not take on the stature of the events in rubber, steel, and autos in 1936 and 1937, it was nonetheless real and significant for Ray-O-Vac's workers. And it encouraged those who conceived of the union as a militant, activist instrument to press their program in the years ahead.

IV.

The Battery Workers and
the Labor Establishment

Before May 1934 the workers at Ray-O-Vac were largely unfamiliar with the trade union movement. Their ability to establish and maintain the union in the face of the company's efforts to cripple or discredit it enabled them to begin serious efforts at collective bargaining with Ray-O-Vac. In many respects, however, it was the task of defining their relationship to the broader labor movement that posed the most significant and difficult problems for these fledgling unionists.

If to ordinary workers the union helped to achieve minimum levels of income and security, a handful of activists found in it an outlet for their energies and enthusiasms. The Depression of the 1930s had hit the American working class with devastating impact, and for many young people of humble origins its worst feature was its denial of hopes for intellectual, social, or occupational advance. Gregory Wallig, who was a charter member of FLU 18456 in Kenosha, followed a course typical of many of his generation. A young man when hard times came, in 1933 Wallig found himself back in the Simmons Furniture Company factory in Kenosha, earning less than he had as a temporarily employed youngster five years before. He had never thought of spending his life in the factory. "Like everyone else in those days," he mused years later, "I was going to write the great American novel." But, with his ambitions dashed and with a family to provide for, he resigned himself to life in the working class, scraped up the three dollars necessary for initiation, and joined the union, eventually to become its president and an AFL organizer.[1]

Amid unemployment, deteriorating housing and living conditions, and routine, deadening jobs, unionism offered many an outlet for oratorical, intellectual, and organizational talents. It enabled young men and women to voice their passionate concerns for social justice. It served as a vehicle for idealism, leadership, and political involvement. Union meetings provided a forum; negotiations with management enabled activists to test their abilities; conventions and conferences broadened horizons, putting workers in touch with kindred souls from around the state and nation. The rising tide of trade unionism in the 1930s, especially in the yeasty, grass-roots federal unions of Wisconsin, enabled these eager activists to combine development of their individual talents with a broad and proud heritage of working-class struggle and achievement.[2]

William Skaar, who for more than thirty-five years was the dominant presence in the union, found the labor movement a heady and exciting experience, although his career as a local union leader was also marked with much bitterness and frustration. Born of Norwegian stock, Skaar was raised and educated in Staughton, Wisconsin, ten miles from Madison. His father worked in a local wagon factory, and Skaar, after graduating from high school in 1918, took various industrial jobs in southern Wisconsin and northern Illinois before permanently joining Ray-O-Vac's labor force in the 1920s. His sister, Nora, became the plant nurse and eventually married Selmer Rorge, a prominent company executive. Although Skaar took occasional extension courses through the University of Wisconsin and although from time to time he left the company or accepted a position in its management hierarchy, he spent almost his entire working life as a Ray-O-Vac employee. The formation of the union in 1934 occurred while he was recuperating from an illness in a Madison hospital; he joined upon returning to work and quickly became a dynamic and vigorous leader in its affairs.[3]

Skaar's own background had included no trade unionism, but he welcomed its appearance. He had always regarded the company as arrogant and arbitrary, and felt unionism made good sense in an industry characterized by low wages and unpleasant working conditions. Skaar quickly demonstrated his energy and articulateness and in 1935 won election as vice-president of 19587. His vigorous defense of trade union principles in the 1936 showdown, when he and the local president McCutchin were fired, confirmed his status as leader, and throughout the 1930s and early 1940s he was elected to positions of local leadership as well as to membership on various state and regional bodies representing battery workers and members of federal unions. At the same time, however, he found the AFL and the cautious work force at Ray-O-Vac constraining. He continually pressed the cause of industrial unionism and political activism, but often found the AFL establishment more concerned with the sensibilities of the craft unions and the specter of the CIO than with forging a militant, aggressive program. Acerbic, blunt, and stubborn, Skaar rankled both some of the more cautious members of 19587 and AFL and WSFL functionaries. For his part, he frequently saw himself the victim of red-baiting and bureaucracy, while some of the other unionists at Ray-O-Vac regarded him as didactic and headstrong. A fellow FLU activist depicted Skaar as more of a "scolder" than a "leader," with no "troops" to follow him. To AFL Regional Director David Sigman, however, Skaar and his fellow activist Gerald Lochner were extremely valuable, effective leaders, passionately committed to the union and properly concerned with linking it to political concerns. In light of the apathy and fickleness so often characteristic of rank-and-file workers, men like Skaar were irreplaceable, Sigman felt.[4]

As 19587 found its place in the labor movement of the 1930s and early 1940s, Skaar continually pleaded, advocated, and instructed, seeking to broaden the horizons of his coworkers and, indirectly, those of the labor establishment of the state and nation. He voiced the concerns of industrial production workers, which jostled uneasily against the craft proclivities of the AFL. He and others like him sought to enhance the status of the federal labor unions within the federation. At times they even raised the possibility of joining the rebel CIO. All of these activities at times distressed or irritated the leadership of the AFL and WSFL, but in none were Skaar and his supporters substantially successful. Thus, David Sigman, while acknowledging that the outspokenness and stubbornness of Skaar and Lochner at times made things uncomfortable, felt that they were never a serious threat to the AFL because, in the end, they needed the union, for personal and practical reasons, as much as the labor movement needed them.[5]

Not all those who rose to positions of influence in 19587's affairs shared Skaar's restless militancy. In sharp contrast was the union career of Max Onsager. A prominent unionist at Ray-O-Vac for almost forty years, Onsager balanced active involvement in the union with sober caution and careful assessment of realistic goals. Born in 1903 in a log cabin near Hillsboro, Wisconsin, Onsager, like Skaar, was of Norwegian descent. As a young man, he ran the family's eighty-acre farm in western Wisconsin for three years, before leaving for Madison in 1923. There, after working briefly with the Chicago and North Western Railroad, he took a permanent job at Ray-O-Vac in 1924. For forty-seven years, Onsager, after a stint in laboratory mixing, was a solderer and spent much of his working life operating soldering and testing machines. Tall and quiet, with a sly sense of humor, Onsager was an early activist, serving on the Grievance Committee and other union posts off and on for over thirty-five years. In 1945, he was elected president of 19587. Throughout his career as a production worker and trade unionist, Onsager showed caution, sober judgment, and an intense desire to find common ground between management and labor. Never particularly vocal or flamboyant in local or state labor affairs, he worked quietly and judiciously, soothing ruffled feelings here, making constructive suggestions to management there. Although a far cry from the angry shop-level militant frequently seen as typical of the labor movement in the 1930s, Onsager proved a steadfast labor man whose views and style frequently struck a responsive chord among other employees.[6]

Men such as Skaar and Onsager, together with other early activists such as Evelyn Gotzion, William McCutchin, and Gerald Lochner, provided local leadership in the early days of the union's existence. From the beginning, however, the federal labor union was inextricably bound up with the larger labor movement. The union's federal charter, the unique circumstances of the energetic Wisconsin State Federation of Labor, and the sense of legalism and structure that permeated the AFL itself very much shaped and conditioned the activities of these local leaders.

Ray-O-Vac workers, like the bulk of their counterparts surging into unions in basic production industries in 1933 and 1934, fit into no neat jurisdictional category. The great majority were unskilled or semiskilled assembly line workers, many of whom were women. These battery workers, like their peers in the automobile, auto parts, rubber, and other industries, found none of the powerful national unions* willing to devote suffi-

*More precisely, one should speak of the "national and international unions," with the term "international" generally denoting the presence of Canadian members. For brevity's sake, the term "national unions" will be used throughout to indicate unions affiliated with the AFL other than the directly affiliated bodies, such as the federal labor unions and local trade unions, which had purely local membership.

cient time and effort to organize and service them. Their only choice was to affiliate through federal labor unions directly with the American Federation of Labor. It was their membership in a federal labor union and its attendant problems that shaped the Ray-O-Vac workers' early relationship to the labor movement per se.

Circumstances made Wisconsin particularly hospitable to the emergence and flourishing of federal labor unions. In Kenosha, Racine, Milwaukee, Janesville, Manitowoc, Two Rivers, Madison, and smaller cities, federal unions had arisen shortly after the establishment of the NRA. Wisconsin contained several industries—metal furniture, brass fittings, auto parts, aluminum, batteries, mechanical pens and pencils—that fell somewhere between the jurisdictions of the AFL crafts and the purview of such rising industrial unions as the auto workers, rubber workers, and electrical workers. Moreover, Henry Ohl, president of the Wisconsin State Federation of Labor, had actively encouraged the formation of federal unions and remained a friend of industrial organization, supported by AFL industrial unions strong in the state such as the pulp and sulphite workers, the paper makers, and the boot and shoe workers. In addition, David Sigman was particularly sympathetic to the federal unions, regarding them as progressive, grassroots organizations, providing a core around which sentiment in favor of industrial organization in the AFL could form. Sigman frequently protected the federal unions from raids by the craft unions and zealously presented their views to the AFL hierarchy. By the late 1930s, the FLUs were also serving as bulwarks against an aggressive Wisconsin CIO, holding workers in mass production industries who might otherwise have been lost due to the ignorance and highhandedness of the crafts. At A. O. Smith Manufacturing Company and International Harvester in Milwaukee, Parker Pen in Janesville, Trane Company in La Cross, Aluminum Company of America plants along Lake Michigan, American Brass in Milwaukee, and about two dozen additional locations around the state, federal unions by the mid-1930s constituted a vigorous and often articulate center of industrial union sentiment within the WSFL and the AFL itself. Thus, at the state federation's annual convention in 1930 hardly any federal unionist appeared, but at the 1935 gathering in Appleton, delegates from directly affiliated locals accounted for well over one-third of the represented membership.[7]

Despite their vigor in Wisconsin, however, federal labor unions were generally considered anomalous appendages to the AFL. On the one hand, they were the AFL's response to the constant challenge to organize mass production workers in industrial unions. At the same time, their historic role had been to serve as temporary units whose primary function was to dole out newly organized workers to the appropriate craft unions. Until 1933, the AFL issued relatively few federal charters, much preferring to leave the task of organizing to the national unions. But the demands for organization that followed passage of the National Industrial Recovery Act in 1933 found many con- stituent unions unwilling or unable to seize the opportunity. Beset by jurisdictional conflicts, weakened by the Depression, fearful of dilution with unstable and unskilled hordes, and concerned lest a sudden influx of new members weaken their grips on the respective union bureaucracies, most craft union leaders responded to demands for organization weakly if at all.

As a consequence, the AFL issued federal charters at an unprecedented rate. But workers receiving these charters found themselves caught in a double bind. The national unions, while skeptical of the qualities of the mass of new unionists, by no means wanted to waive future jurisdictional claims. National unions frequently criticized the issuance of federal charters, contending that they infringed on traditional jurisdictional claims or constituted de facto dual unionism. Some national unions moved quickly—critics said ruthlessly—to claim mem- bers of their crafts from the defenseless new unions. The upshot was to put the federal unions in the middle of incessant jurisdictional squabbling, a circumstance that irritated many of the new unionists and convinced them further of their need to organize on an industrial basis.

At the same time, the federal unions dealt directly with and through the AFL in their initial legal proceedings, organizing drives, and negotiating sessions. The AFL, however, was not a labor union; its bureaucracy was not geared to do the things that the staffs of national unions normally did. Conceiving of the federal unions in part as an answer to the demand for industrial unionism and in part as holding bodies for the future claims of the nationals, the AFL did not eagerly shoulder the burden of bargaining, organizing, and conducting strikes. Ever fearful of antagonizing the national unions, yet deeply involved in the day-to-day management of the affairs of hundreds of new unions, the federation proved hesitant and unsure. While these new unionists impatiently sought immediate gains and aggressive laborite activism, the established labor movement responded with cautious advice, jurisdictional quibbling, and bewildered leadership.

The federal unions occupied a special place within the AFL structure. The federation's constitution conceived of them as direct affiliates, different in most respects from the local unions of the nationals. Since the AFL had to provide the federal unions with legal advice, negotiating service, and information and research—functions normally performed for local unions by the staffs of their respective nationals—it exacted a higher per capita tax from a federal union than from a national union. Under the constitutional regulations prevailing in 1934, and modified only in detail thereafter, the national unions paid the federation one cent per member per month, while the federal unions paid the parent body 25 percent of its monthly dues collection.

To many federal unionists, this dues differential was disproportionately high. While it was true that the AFL provided the services usually performed for locals by the nationals, many federal unionists felt that the AFL did not perform these functions very well. The AFL had no designated legal, research, or organizational staff specifically earmarked for the federal unions. Most AFL service was provided through state or city federation representatives, with a relatively small number of central staff organizers helping out. The primary functions of the state federations, however, lay in the field of lobbying, political action, and coordination of activities among the national unions. Since most state representatives (and most AFL organizers) were recruited from the ranks of the national unions, it was quite natural that they would stress these functions and relegate the concerns of the federal unions to secondary status. AFL officials denied this charge as frequently as federal unionists made it.

Federal unionists had other grievances as well. Until 1902, there had been no strike fund available to them, despite their heavy per capita taxes. Even with the constitutional requirement that the federation set aside 5 percent of dues collected from federal unions as a war chest, the process of receiving strike sanction was cumbersome and heavily weighted toward appeasing the federation's penchant for caution as opposed to local unionists' pressing complaints. Moreover, a federal union had to maintain itself in good standing for a year after charter issuance to qualify for modest strike benefits. Thus, despite the fact that unprecedented grass-roots militancy and the impatience of production workers were creating the new unions, their very charters guaranteed a certain amount of frustration born of this bias toward caution and orderliness.

Federal unionists also complained that the AFL wanted to break them up, to parcel out their members to the greedy national unions as soon as possible. Thus, while federal locals in a number of industries, including the battery trade, constantly sought some means of mutual aid and national organization, the AFL sought to discourage these efforts and to persuade them to acquiesce in takeover by the crafts. Nor could representatives of the federal unions marshal much strength within the AFL, for both the annual convention and the Executive Council were dominated by the large and influential national unions. No representative from the federal unions ever sat on the Executive Council, and the directly affiliated bodies found it impossible to send the thousands of delegates to national conventions that would have been necessary if they were to exercise their full voting strength. Typically, in view of the overwhelming preponderance of national union votes, only a handful of federal union delegates ever bothered to attend.[8]

Federal unions such as 19587 in Wisconsin received service from both the State Federation of Labor and the AFL regional director's office, both of which were housed in Milwaukee. Throughout most of the 1930s and 1940s, the regional directors were men closely associated with the WSFL and hence the two offices functioned in tandem. The regional director and state federation organizers traveled extensively throughout the state, addressing meetings, helping with negotiations, and seeking to resolve internal problems. The AFL's Washington headquarters, however, provided relatively little day-to-day support. Despite the rapid expansion of the labor movement in the 1930s, the AFL persisted in office routines and research processes reminiscent of the horse-and-buggy days of trade unionism. In particular, federal unions, which had no international representatives or research staffs of their own, complained of the sporadic and even eccentric responses to requests for information about comparative wage rates, corporate profits, and industrial conditions that came out of the AFL

Research Department, headed by old-time federation function-ary, Florence C. Thorne.[9]

FLUs in Wisconsin had less cause for complaint about the organizers who serviced their unions. David Sigman was a particular favorite among federal unionists. Born in Polish Russia early in the century, he had come to America as a small child when his family settled in Two Rivers. He was a short man with a vigorous constitution and quick intelligence. Though financial problems forced him to leave the University of Wisconsin after one semester, Sigman nonetheless retained an active interest in social problems and economic analysis. While in Madison, he observed sessions of the state legislature and became convinced that he could be as effective a lawmaker as were those in the chamber. When Sigman returned to Two Rivers in 1931 he ran successfully as a La Follette Progressive, becoming one of Wisconsin's youngest representatives, as well as one of its few Jewish lawmakers.

Sigman's interest in economic and social questions found expression in the legislature, and the resurgence of the labor movement in 1933 and 1934 provided an outlet for his abilities. He accompanied Henry Ohl in 1934 when the WSFL president addressed a mass meeting of aluminum operatives and other workers in Two Rivers, thrilling to the sense of mass activism and social rebirth that suffused labor's rise. Ohl found that, while many workers were willing to sign up for a federal charter, he could find no one willing to assume the new union's presidency. Sigman, a well-known and respected figure in the community, agreed to serve temporarily in that capacity, and thus launched his career in the labor movement. Shortly after, AFL President William Green asked him to help the regional director, Paul Smith, with organizing work; in 1937 Sigman himself was appointed regional director.

The lawmaker-organizer had a particular affection for the federal unions. As a man outside the labor establishment, he found the imperious craft unionists often callous and indifferent to the plight of workers in mass production industries. He saw the federal unions as vehicles for progressive political action as well as repositories of vigorous rank-and-file involvement in trade unionism. His experience with Ohl in Two Rivers deeply impressed him with the potentialities of the FLUs. He witnessed at firsthand the killing of two pickets and the wounding of scores more in the strike of FLU 18545 against the Kohler Company.

Throughout his tenure as regional director he sought to protect the federal unions from dismemberment by established national unions and proved a vigorous and popular representative among local unionists.[10]

Sigman's successor as regional director, Jacob F. Friedrick, was of German extraction and had immigrated from the Austro-Hungarian Empire in 1905. A machinist by trade, Friedrick joined the International Association of Machinists (IAM) in 1913 and served as business agent for Milwaukee District Lodge No. 10 from 1919 to 1929. He was also active in the Milwaukee Federated Trades Council and the Socialist party, and served as a reporter and labor editor for the *Milwaukee Leader*. He compensated for his lack of formal education with a rigorous program of self-instruction in history, law, and economics. A leader in workers' education in the state, he conducted courses and participated in the founding of the University of Wisconsin's School for Workers in Industry. Late in his career he was appointed to the University of Wisconsin Board of Regents and served as chairman of the board in 1961 and 1962. Although his background was in the craft union environment of Milwaukee, Friedrick strongly supported industrial organization and as late as 1937 urged compromise with the dissident CIO unions. Though an ardent AFL champion who, once the split became permanent, pressed the federation's cause vigorously, Friedrick enjoyed a reputation even among his opponents for judiciousness, vigor, and integrity.[11]

Down through the years, the WSFL employed a number of exceptionally able and energetic organizers and representatives. Andrew Biemiller, whose itinerary often took him to the meetings of 19587, was twice elected to the United States House of Representatives and eventually became legislative director of the AFL-CIO. Walter Uphoff, whose activism in state politics, the union label movement, and labor publications put him in frequent contact with Ray-O-Vac unionists, became a prominent labor economist and author. Charles Heymanns, a native of Luxembourg, served for many years as a WSFL organizer and AFL representative, earning a reputation as an ebullient, ubiquitous labor spokesman. Always eager to be on the firing line, Heymanns drove around the state in his Nash, with the glove compartment and his coat pockets stuffed with rosters, contracts, and other union business. Heymanns, remarked WSFL President George Haberman, knew everything worth knowing about labor affairs in Wisconsin; he was a "walking filing cabinet." One of 19587's members recalled Heymanns, who often advised the local, as a "two pitcher" man, for his speeches usually lasted through at least two containers of water. Heymanns' *speeches*, mused one of his oldest friends in the labor movement affectionately, were not lengthy, but his *conclusions* certainly took a long time.[12]

Throughout the early history of 19587—indeed, through-out its entire career—the membership was sharply divided in its assessment of the value of the support and service that the AFL provided. Clearly, the support from the AFL, especially through the Wisconsin State Federation of Labor and the Madison Federation of Labor, was crucial in getting the union started. By the late 1930s, however, a substantial segment of the membership was growing impatient and resentful over what they viewed as the AFL's conservatism, caution, and inadequate treatment of federal unions. In 1934 and 1935, the inexperi-enced unionists tended to be deferential and amenable to the initiatives and recommendations of AFL representatives. Once 19587 was firmly established, however, its members began to question AFL policies and to dissent from bargaining recom-mendations. Increasingly embroiled with the AFL officialdom over local issues and over their efforts to expand the influence of battery workers and federal unions within AFL councils, the militant leaders of the late 1930s also had to contend with a significant faction in the federal union that disapproved of their efforts.[13]

Veteran members of the union disagree as to the efficacy of AFL support for 19587 in its early days. Certainly, the physical presence of a labor temple and the availability of volunteer organizers and speakers from the Madison Federation of Labor provided needed early encouragement. In early meetings, the new unionists heard speeches about the structure and functions of the AFL, the benefits and obligations of union membership, the intricacies of state and national labor law, and the turbulent labor scene of the summer and early fall of 1934. Such promi-nent figures in Wisconsin labor as Arnold F. Zander, a pioneer-ing organizer of public employees; J. J. Handley, State Federa-tion of Labor secretary-treasurer; Ed Hall, a leader in the emerging United Automobile Workers; and Paul Smith, a Milwaukee-based AFL representative, addressed meetings and counseled with the membership. Hall, Smith, Sigman, and

Judge Joseph Padway, AFL legal adviser, sat in with 19587's bargaining and grievance committees in early negotiations with Ray-O-Vac. On two occasions, in 1936 and 1941, the membership expressed enthusiastic appreciation for Sigman's help in the settlement of disputes with the company. Only once during these years, in 1936, did the union request strike sanction from the AFL, which it received but did not have to use. To some veteran union activists such as Max Onsager, who served on the Grievance Committee almost continuously from 1934, AFL service was prompt, straightforward, and invaluable to the new federal union. Indeed, to Onsager and other devotees of the federal union, the only problem with direct AFL affiliation was the desire of the federation to terminate it and to have the union surrender its charter so that it could be absorbed by one of the national unions. To these people, such a move would have ended the autonomy and local control they felt they enjoyed as a federal union.[14]

To others, such as Skaar, federal status and indeed the whole AFL structure was unsatisfactory. These activists argued that federal unions paid out far more in dues than they received in services. They found the AFL staff tardy and inadequate in responding to their requests for research on the battery industry. They were shocked to learn that they had to pay for the services of an AFL legal representative who helped them draw up a contract with management. They found the representatives from the WSFL and the AFL arbitrary and unsympathetic to their problems, far more eager to effect compromise, to avoid unpleasantness, and to cooperate with management than to press for the legitimate demands of the local membership. Skaar, for years the stormy petrel of 19587, found AFL representatives habitually arrogant and highhanded, uninterested in the affairs of the small federal local unless its membership threatened militant action. In Skaar's view, AFL neglect and caution were coupled on occasion with collusion with management, personal attacks on local dissidents, and blatant red-baiting.[15]

If prominent members of 19587 disagreed as to the quality of AFL service, they also differed over the proper role of their union in the labor movement as a whole. Many members were content with federal status and with their direct AFL affiliation, seeking no wider influence or broader association. Although they willingly participated in regional and state conferences of battery workers and federal unions, they did so in a spirit of genial cooperation and mutual friendship and conviviality. They were skeptical of efforts to create consolidated battery workers' or federal union bodies designed to press a militant program.

Over the years, the conferences and councils of battery workers and federal unions that 19587 participated in did in fact usually reflect this moderate, cautious stance. Skaar and other activists, however, sought continually to create more aggressive organizations. Motivated in part by the practical desire to protect and improve their own wage structure and in part by a genuine desire to proselytize, 19587's activists played a major role in efforts to organize the dry cell battery industry. They made numerous visits to Burgess Battery workers in Freeport, Illinois, and to the General Dry Battery Company plant in Dubuque, Iowa. They kept in close contact with Eveready workers in Cleveland until the Ohioans abandoned their federal charter and joined the National Radio and Allied Trades Council, forerunner of the CIO United Electrical, Radio, and Machine Workers, in 1936. They also sought to bolster existing unions in other Ray-O-Vac plants, especially one in Lancaster, Ohio, which made products similar to those turned out in Madison. Throughout the middle and late 1930s, small auto caravans of Ray-O-Vac workers frequently wound their way to these battery centers, hoping to organize the unorganized.[16]

In addition, the activist element wanted to expand the influence of the newly organized production workers within the councils of the AFL. Keenly aware of the secondary status of the federal unions, they moved on two fronts to enhance their power. One effort was to form a battery workers' council as a means of exchanging information, coordinating contract negotiations, and asserting their common interests in the AFL. Skaar and others active in the battery councils hoped eventually for the establishment of a national battery workers' union, organized along industrial lines, that would take its place alongside the militant unions of production workers that were emerging in other sectors of American industry in the 1930s.

The other effort was to create a council or conference of federal labor unions within the AFL. Aside from merely coordinating activities and exchanging information, such a body could become a bold and aggressive force. Since federal unions were almost by definition industrial unions, a strong organization among them could push the AFL into a more progressive stance and could thereby encourage further organization of industrial workers. At the least, a vigorous federal union body could counteract the raids by the national unions on federal unions and might achieve a greater voice for the FLUs at the AFL convention and in state and local federations and central bodies. At the 1937 convention of the AFL in Denver, Skaar worked with a group of federal unionists who sought to change the constitution to recognize the growth in membership and importance of the federal unions. Defeated, he and other 19587 activists continually pressed their claims at state and regional conventions and conferences, but to little avail. Despite the rapid growth of the federal unions in the 1930s, the AFL continued to view them as temporary bodies of new recruits. Certainly the powerful chieftains of the dominant craft unions, while beginning under the goad of the CIO challenge to recognize the need to organize production workers, were not about to allow any shift in the internal balance of power of the federation. Thus, although 19587 members loyally attended various conferences and meetings of federal unions and battery workers, these bodies increasingly assumed the routine consultative character that the local's more moderate members had always favored.[17]

Throughout the first six or seven years, these disagreements simmered beneath the surface, occasionally erupting into acrimony among the members or between the activist faction and city and national AFL representatives. On two occasions, however, 19587 became directly involved in serious disputes with the labor establishment. One began in the mid-1930s, when the local and the Madison Federation of Labor became involved in a series of quarrels that lasted for years. Concurrently, some 19587 leaders initiated contacts with the rebel CIO and thus brought down upon themselves the wrath of the entire AFL hierarchy.

Although representatives of the MFL were instrumental in the birth of the federal union, 19587 members soon wearied of the city central's cautious tutelage. In a 1935 controversy with Ray-O-Vac, for example, the federal union charged that the MFL secretary had arbitrarily taken matters out of its hands and had thereby damaged its bargaining position. In the same year the local and the city body got into an obscure quarrel about responsibilities for maintenance of the Labor Temple. In the spring of 1936, the federal union endured a lengthy and bitter confrontation with the company, with many members convinced that Ray-O-Vac was trying to break the union. Yet in November, Sol Reist, an MFL official, evoked bitter criticism from the local when he printed an advertisement from Ray-O-Vac for the local labor newspaper that extolled the harmonious relationships between the battery concern and organized labor. By early 1937 relations between the union and the MFL had deteriorated, and 19587 eventually withdrew from the city central.[18]

Quite apart from these petty disputes were differences between the union and the MFL concerning the basic principles and purposes of the labor movement. The AFL valued its city centrals, for they constituted its visible presence in communities across the country. Usually dominated by the building trades unions and the teamsters, these bodies often wielded power in local politics. Moreover, they provided the fulcrum for the AFL in its efforts to secure adherence to its rulings on jurisdictional disputes and other interunion controversies. The city centrals were the vital links between the national AFL and the daily world of labor politics, buttressing as they did the Olympian pronouncements of the federation's top leadership with practical implementation. Clearly, in view of their dominance by the craft unions and their carefully nurtured influence in federation affairs and in local politics, these central bodies were little inclined to accommodate themselves to new, inexperienced, and frequently impatient and militant federal unionists.[19]

Thus it was in Madison. From the viewpoint of the activists who led the union in the middle and late 1930s, the MFL and the Dane County Trades Council were rigidly conservative bodies. Whereas 19587 generously supported virtually all local strikes regardless of the workers' affiliation, the city and county bodies refused to help any group of workers remotely tinged with CIO influence. In 1938–39, Skaar recalls, the city central refused even to aid locked out Ray-O-Vac workers until local newspaper coverage shamed it into token support. Federal union enthusiasts, eager to have the labor movement expand and broaden its ideological and organizational base, found the craft leaders of the central to be cautious and dilatory, more concerned about preserving their local political influence and their hold on the area labor movement than with social justice or recruiting new members. In 1939, Lochner declared, "It has often been said that the Madison Federation of Labor is the most reactionary city central . . . in the state . . .; I would amend this and say in the entire country."[20]

The challenge of the CIO beginning in 1936 also strained the relationship of 19587 with established AFL bodies, local and national. Battery workers felt a natural kinship with such emerging CIO unions as the United Rubber Workers, the United Auto Workers, and the United Electrical, Radio, and Machine Workers (UE). Not only were these industrial unions of production workers, but they had grown at least partly out of federal labor unions established in 1933 and 1934. The auto workers' metamorphosis from separate federal unions to an Auto Workers' Council to a separate, militant industrial union paralleled the hopes that many members of 19587 harbored for battery workers.

From the outset of the open AFL-CIO schism in the summer of 1936, 19587 supported the claims of the industrial unionists. In August, the union protested to the AFL Executive Council against that body's recent decision to suspend the CIO unions and urged the AFL "to cooperate with the CIO in organizing the steel and rubber industries." The local also sought to rally support for industrial unionism in Madison and the surrounding area. It contacted nearby local unions and presented a motion before the MFL in support of the CIO organizations, a move that further exacerbated the federal union's shaky relationship with the conservative city central.[21]

Nor was the union's support confined to verbal declarations. The union extended fraternal greetings to new CIO locals in the nearby plants of Kipp Chemical, Gisholt Machinery, and Burgess Battery, supporting their efforts to gain entry into the city central, a move that the MFL leadership defeated. In the summer of 1937, 19587 sent pickets to aid striking CIO Burgess Battery workers and pressed motions in the MFL calling for similar expressions of support from all Madison unions. On June 11, 1937, the local membership defiantly approved a resolution "not to pay assessment to A.F.L. in their fight against C.I.O.," a stand that the AFL later forced it to reverse.[22]

Throughout the late 1930s, 19587 members kept personally informed about CIO developments, in spite of AFL displeasure. In late summer 1936, the local chose Skaar as its delegate to a state CIO meeting in Milwaukee, and Skaar went despite the federation's excommunication of the rebel unions. A particularly vigorous proponent of the CIO, Skaar hoped that the local membership could be brought around to eventual affiliation with a CIO union such as the UE. Sometime in the late 1930s, he journeyed east to confer with UE officers James B. Carey and James Matles and to visit AFL President Green. He returned further convinced of the hopeless conservatism and inadequacy of the AFL and of the militancy and relevance of the CIO and UE.[23]

Despite its sympathy for the principles and activities of the CIO, however, 19587 remained with the AFL. An influential group of activists opposed affiliation with any national union, especially one bearing the stigma of the CIO. Skaar was a respected leader, frequently elected president of the local, but many who otherwise supported him feared that the company would respond to CIO affiliation and a militant program of action by moving operations to its Lancaster, Ohio, plant. Moreover, AFL representatives bore down hard on those with CIO sympathies. In June 1939 Representative Sigman noted, "It has come to our attention that the officers of . . . 19587 are toying with the idea of working together with the C.I.O. organizations in the battery industry." Together with AFL Representative Biemiller and WSFL President Ohl, Sigman squelched this effort abruptly. At the local's meeting of June 16, 1939, he advised the officers that the federation would "not tolerate any C.I.O. activities." Skaar felt that AFL officials resorted to chicanery, intimidation, and red-baiting to discredit those who favored common action with the CIO unions or who even tried through a vigorous battery council movement to strengthen the position of the battery workers within the AFL.[24]

V.
Troubled Times, 1936–40

In Wisconsin no less than in the country as a whole the late 1930s were years of militancy and ferment.[1] The launching of the CIO, the dramatic strikes and organizing campaigns, and the conflict between the rival labor organizations made the American labor scene turbulent and dynamic. Federal Labor Union 19587 shared in the militancy and activism that American workers displayed in these years, as it attempted to follow its successful establishment with growth and development. The course that the union followed in the period from 1936 to 1940 reflects both the successes and limitations of the rank-and-file militancy that has loomed so large in the annals of the 1930s.

Journalists, participants, and historians have long been interested in the character of local activism and its relation to the unions' leadership. The major narrative accounts of the 1930s by Walter Galenson, Irving Bernstein, and Sidney Fine vividly describe the uncommon vitality of rank-and-file protest, while many contemporary participants and observers stress the explosiveness of the phenomenon. To some commentators, this dynamism represents the true legacy of the 1930s. Such writers as Staughton Lynd, Len De Caux, Farrel Dobbs, and James Matles see the eventual emergence of a centralized CIO and a revived AFL as destructive of the fierce democracy and shop-level vigor that originally characterized the upheaval of the 1930s.[2] Thus far, however, little attention has been directed to the experiences of workers in local unions as they struggled not only to create their unions but to maintain and develop them in the stormy years before World War II.[3] Although the specific circumstances confronting the members of FLU 19587 were unique, the tensions between militancy and caution, activism and apathy, and leadership and membership were common to all unions born in the 1930s.

Having established itself in the mid-thirties by virtue of its early enthusiasm and steadfastness, 19587 faced major splits over its direction and development after the 1936 dispute. One group of activists envisaged the union as a militant, aggressive champion of justice in society as well as on the shop floor. A second group, equally active in the affairs of the union, saw the union as an agent of conciliation and understanding, denying the legitimacy of political action or social crusading as proper functions. Throughout the late 1930s, these groups waged a ragged battle for control. Although the militant faction led the union throughout most of this period, rank-and-filers' enthusiasm for their aggressive programs eventually waned in the light of Ray-O-Vac's hostility, the AFL's opposition, and their own lack of commitment to the cause of progressive unionism. By 1940, conservatives were in control of the union's leadership, with the militants at least temporarily elbowed aside.[4]

Despite the internal dispute of its early years, the union served as a focal point for social and cultural activities, a function that helped to solidify the workers. Madison's working class in the 1930s, while somewhat isolated from the rest of the city residentially, bore little resemblance to the classic proletarian stereotypes. The spread of education, the physical mobility provided by the automobile, and the intrusions of packaged culture from the electronic media ensured that the union per se could never assume the dimensions of a full-fledged class subculture. There is no evidence of socialist study groups or evangelistic singing of the defiant protest songs of laborite legend among the annals of 19587.[5]

The union did provide educational and cultural activities for the sophisticated, urban, consumer-oriented American workers in the 1930s. It regularly entertained guest speakers from the labor movement, the state and local political scene, and the university. Meetings were frequently followed by dances, complete with "lunch" and brew, a sure attraction for beer-loving Wisconsinites. The union sponsored bowling tournaments, baseball and kittenball teams, picnics, and keno parties. Indeed, on one occasion desire for victory in an important game led the membership to compromise its laborite consciousness: on July 7, 1936, it voted affirmatively on the motion that the "organization accept a pitcher outside of the union to go with the ball team to Beaver Dam." The social committee tapped the local talent market to provide edifying entertainment for the members. Music for one party was supplied by the Seven Dutch Girls; on another occasion those with presumably more elevated tastes were rewarded with "entertainment . . . furnished by Miss Helen Dedrickson's School of Dancing."[6]

These activities, however, absorbed relatively little of the workers' free time. The radio, movies, the automobile, and professional spectator sports provided the bulk of their diversion. For the men, hunting and fishing helped to mitigate factory routine. Both men and women invested enormous energy in the acquisition, refurbishment, and continual improvement of their homes. Well-trimmed lawns, carefully swept sidewalks, lovingly tended backyard gardens, and neat, though modest, internal appointments characterized the residences of working-class Madison. Even in the doleful thirties, and more so in the more prosperous forties, battery workers foresaw a brighter future for their children and determined that their own hard work would provide educational and occupational opportunities for their offspring. In short, although the union filled an obvious economic need and provided a certain amount of camaraderie and cohesiveness, it could not compete with Hollywood and the Mutual Network, to say nothing of home and family, for cultural and personal allegiance.[7]

The attitude of 19587's membership toward political action also reflected the limited nature of the battery workers' consciousness of class interests. While sponsorship of athletic and social affairs was often popular, those who advocated political action on the part of the union frequently encountered opposition. To many of 19587's members, politics was a purely private affair, no more relevant to union concerns than was religion. Others, temporarily in the majority in the late 1930s, pressed for a vigorous program of political education and action, urging the membership to express itself on a broad range of social issues.

Under the energetic leadership of Lochner and Skaar, the union endorsed progressive political aspirants, expressed support for federal medical care and housing legislation, urged a boycott of Japanese goods, and contributed to various civil libertarian and labor defense funds. Skaar frequently took time at meetings to read and discuss newspaper articles on current affairs, hoping to alert his fellow workers to the connections between their immediate problems and the broader social and economic context. Other members, however, resented this intrusion of social and political advocacy and castigated Skaar for prolonging meetings with such irrelevant subjects. Thus, although the minute books and correspondence of the union for the 1930s reveal considerable social consciousness, the union never developed a consistent political stance and over the years the antipolitical faction grew stronger.[8]

The two and a half years following the 1936 affray proved the highpoint of militancy and social concern in the local. Although McCutchin left Ray-O-Vac and the union late in 1936, Skaar, Lochner, and other activists continued to hold key offices and to shape the response of the union to the company, to the social environment, and to developments in the labor movement. In 1937 the organization won a modified union shop contract, while the Grievance Committee bargained with more confidence with management. It was during this period too that 19587 vocally criticized AFL attacks on the CIO and actively investigated possibilities of joining the dissident federation. Within the AFL, Skaar and others pressed ahead with their campaign to strengthen the federal unions and to form a battery council. Although thwarted at the 1937 AFL convention in Denver, 19587 delegates found it "a great pleasure to work with other progressive delegates from progressive unions." Local and state AFL officials disapproved of the Ray-O-Vac local's chronic dissidence and activism, but fellow unionists applauded their willingness to contribute time and money in strikes and organizing campaigns. "If all the groups in Madison would cooperate in such ways," observed a striking packing house employee in a letter to FLU 19587, "we would have a true Union city." He went on to say that 19587's offer of financial assistance and help on the picket line had "taught the new members . . . the value of organized labor."[9]

The progressives in 19587 coupled their advanced social and political views with shop-level activism. They argued grievances aggressively and constantly attacked Ray-O-Vac's reputation for low wages. They regarded the company as highly profitable and felt that Ray-O-Vac could finance both adequate wages and needed retooling directly out of earned income. Skaar and other vocal unionists felt that the company had fought genuine collective bargaining for years; now that the union had proved itself, its leaders owed it to the members to press vigorously for more adequate wages and benefits. In Skaar's view, shop-level militancy went hand in hand with his and his colleagues' broad definition of the function of the union.[10]

Those in the more moderate group resented the militant

leaders and were at best indifferent to their political and ideological concerns. Many active unionists considered Skaar's efforts in behalf of a federal labor union council and in support of a national battery workers' union to be primarily motivated by personal ambition. Skaar, they felt, wanted to land a good job in whatever organization resulted from his efforts. In addition, many battery workers suspected that the frequent trips made by Skaar and other leaders to promote organization of other battery plants, to further federal labor union unity, or to participate in state and national AFL affairs were devoted more to beer parties and philandering than to union matters. These criticisms, together with continuing resentment over the political and "educational" enthusiasms of the militants, were a constant brake on the social unionism that the activist element championed.[11]

Probably the most serious split in the union resulted from conflicting perceptions of the company and of the gains that union workers could legitimately expect. Militants scoffed at Ray-O-Vac's frequent threats to move operations and its equally frequent bemoaning of its competitive position in the battery industry. Many unionists, however, did not share this scorn. Some, including elected officers, had frequent informal contact with company executives. When foremen and managers spoke earnestly in East Side taverns and bowling alleys of the company's spiraling costs and deteriorating markets, union members listened sympathetically. Over the years, many Ray-O-Vac employees, particularly older workers and women who were not their families' primary breadwinners, had come to believe that Ray-O-Vac stayed in Madison in part because of the firm's loyalty to its workers and community. Though they never quite embraced the cozy view of employee relations that the company had tried to inculcate in the 1920s, many workers felt that the company had been generally forthright and honorable in its dealings with them. They were little inclined to support a union leadership which appeared to be belligerent and insensitive to the business problems that their neighbors and bowling partners in management faced.[12]

Thus, differences in perception combined with differences in conception. To Skaar and the militants, it was the union's duty to wage an aggressive battle for labor's rights. The good union man or woman fought every grievance and pressed a reluctant company for every penny in wages and benefits. At the same time, it awakened workers to the need to join their efforts to those of other workers in all manner of progressive endeavors. To Max Onsager and many other members of 19587, however, it was the union's job to conciliate, to gain insight into the problems of the company, to serve as a vehicle for communication and understanding. The union, in the view of many of its active members, was neither a fighting battalion nor a political caucus. Rather, it was a means of alleviating the occasional difficulties of two groups of people who had much in common and little reason for animosity.[13]

Rank-and-file members followed an ambivalent course in regard to these sharply different conceptions of the union's role. There is little in the extensive records of 19587 that directly speaks to the specific attitudes of the vast majority of those who worked at Ray-O-Vac and who paid dues to the union. For years, while they elected militants and moderates simultaneously, they appeared to perceive the union as neither the progressive tool envisaged by Skaar nor the primarily conciliatory body that Onsager advocated. The union was a useful device with which to pry concessions from management, and it could defend a worker in a grievance procedure. It kept the company honest and fought the battles that inarticulate and vulnerable production workers were unable and unwilling to fight individually. Yet, while the rank and file was willing to vote approval of progressive political and social causes and to support militant leadership on bargaining issues, there was little mass backing for the implicit ideology behind this militancy. There were times when grievances had to be fought aggressively and when the company had to be threatened, but it was good also to have available people like Onsager with personal contacts with management functionaries. These union officials knew the language of moderation and could soften the abrasiveness associated with the militants.

Skaar's "educational" efforts never really took hold and the local failed to become a significant political force. In addition, as Skaar himself would observe in later years, most rank-and-file members paid little attention to the daily affairs of the union. The dominant attitude, even in the tempestuous 1930s, he recalled, was "let Bill do it." A militant union was indeed a useful weapon, but it was not the central institution in the lives of most Ray-O-Vac workers that it was to William Skaar.

It was not that the rank-and-filers were passive or ill

informed. Rather, they seemed to steer instinctively between the relative extremes represented by the more active leaders. To most Ray-O-Vac workers over the years the union was both a prod and a facilitator. It might threaten fruitfully at times; it might exude understanding and conciliation at times. But it would never be totally the servant of either the militant or the moderate faction.[14]

These conflicts between militants and conservatives, which occupied much of the union members' attention after the 1936 dispute, came to a head in 1938. Negotiations with the company, conducted by the militant bargaining committee led by Skaar and Lochner, reached an impasse that fall. The resulting shutdown of the plant in December eroded support for the militants and ended for the time being the tendency toward social unionism that had been emerging in FLU 19587. Combining to undermine the activist group were three related forces: the hostile attitude of the company toward their uncompromising bargaining posture; the disapproval of state and national AFL representatives; and the uncertainty and caution among the rank and file, fed by the dire warnings of the union's conservative activists.

Company officials, while willing to bargain and to sign contracts with the union, felt that the local officers were unrealistic in their demands. When the militant-oriented Grievance Committee called for substantial wage increases in the summer of 1938, the company flatly refused, contending that unionization of Ray-O-Vac had already raised standards there above those generally prevailing in the industry and had thus weakened its competitive position. Ray-O-Vac officials asserted that their chief competitor, Eveready, had moved aggressively into the production of batteries for portable appliances and radios. Moreover, the Madison executives declared, Eveready's greater capitalization, wider diversity of products, and more extensive marketing opportunities gave it crucial advantages over Ray-O-Vac. If the company was to remain competitive, they argued, it would have to invest heavily in research and retooling. If new lines of products proved profitable, Ray-O-Vac could contemplate wage increases, but meanwhile Madison workers would have to tighten their belts and bear with the company during this difficult time—if they wanted their jobs to remain in the city.[15]

Skaar, Lochner, and many other production workers rejected this line of argument. Although the union had no direct access to company books, these leaders felt that the public information provided in state tax returns revealed large profits, certainly sufficient to finance remodeling without penalizing workers. In the late spring and early summer of 1938, union and management reached an impasse over the terms of a new contract, and at its July 5 meeting the membership voted to authorize a strike in support of its demands for higher wages.[16]

Over the next several months, a deadlock developed. In December, company officials were ready to close down the plant. If the membership did not accept a temporary wage cut while Ray-O-Vac retooled, the company would have to contemplate moving its operations to its more tractable Lancaster, Ohio, facility. Moreover, Cargill made it known that he considered the present Grievance Committee headed by Skaar and Lochner to be irresponsible, jeopardizing the future of the company and employees alike with its belligerent and unrealistic attitude. Ominously, late in the fall of 1938 Ray-O-Vac employees observed equipment and materials being ostentatiously taken from the factory and loaded onto nearby railroad cars, presumably headed for Ohio. Before long it became clear that the company would indeed close down operations in Madison, although workers remained divided in their assessments as to whether the company was merely trying to frighten them with a temporary layoff or if it would in fact move operations permanently out of Madison.[17]

Company threats to shift operations were not new. Ray-O-Vac officials had frequently reminded workers that there was no intrinsic reason for them to remain in Madison. They also criticized 19587 and the labor movement in general for failure to organize other battery concerns, holding that they had to follow a rigorous wage policy so that they could meet the competition that nonunion firms presented. Thus, as they shut down and prepared to move at least some operations to Ohio, company officers felt that they had given fair warning, both in formal meetings with the union and in the many casual contacts they had with their employees. If Ray-O-Vac moved out of Madison, the workers had only their own intransigent leaders to blame.

Many rank-and-filers agreed. Even today, veterans of the union's early years are sharply divided between those who felt the company was bluffing and those who were convinced that it meant to abandon Madison. Onsager, for example, felt that the company was in difficulty in 1938, having lost out on a bid to supply Philco Radio Company with batteries for its new line of portable radios. Onsager, who enjoyed friendly relations with many company officials and invariably found them honest and straightforward, thought that many of the younger members of the union were too impatient and impetuous, unable to appreciate the company's real problems. Even union activists with a less generous assessment of Ray-O-Vac's management admitted the force of the company's complaint about lack of organization in the battery trade. Members of 19587 had for years worked to expand organization in Dubuque, Rockford, Lancaster, and other battery-making centers, but they had little to show for their efforts.[18]

The plant closed down on December 22, 1938. Most members of 19587 found it difficult to find temporary work, and some suspected that Ray-O-Vac may have promoted a kind of informal blacklist among local employers. With unemployment adding to the gloom of a Wisconsin winter, and with little support from the Madison Federation of Labor or from the AFL, some members of the union began to consider the company's criticism of the Grievance Committee. Two prominent unionists met privately with Ray-O-Vac officials and came away convinced of the union's foolishness and of the disastrous leadership provided by Skaar and Lochner. They called for a reconstituted committee, one that would discard the belligerent attitude of the present body. One angry critic lashed out at Skaar, accusing him publicly of personal indiscretions, misuse of union funds, and communist leanings. He reported that it was common knowledge in the working-class areas of the city that Ray-O-Vac was preparing to pull out entirely and that Federal Labor Union 19587's own folly had led to this disaster. This irate unionist, recorded the union's secretary in an uncensored entry of January 6, 1939, "said that Superintendent of Gisholt [Machine Company, a leading Madison firm,] told him that we guys shit in our own nest."[19]

Rank-and-file response was ambivalent, if not downright contradictory. In December, Skaar offered to resign as head of the Grievance Committee. The membership accepted his resignation, but turned around to elect him president of the local. Both votes were close, with the dissident leader gaining the presidency by a scant 16 votes out of 368 ballots cast. At the same time, internal conflict together with the reality of joblessness took their toll. Initially, the union filed charges with the regional office of the National Labor Relations Board, charging the company with interference in the affairs of the union and with discrimination against union members. For a time the membership adhered to this aggressive course, and on January 20, 1939, it once again rejected a company proposal to reopen the plant upon the union's acquiescence to wage cuts. When WSFL representatives advised Skaar to drop the NLRB charges as a gesture of conciliation, he angrily refused, with apparent support from the membership.[20]

In the end, however, the reality of joblessness and the lack of employment opportunities in Madison forced the union to come to terms. WSFL officials, who Onsager accused of having encouraged the local's stubbornness in the first place, eagerly sought a settlement. David Sigman and Andrew Biemiller met repeatedly with Ray-O-Vac officials in early 1939, seeking to have the plant reopened. Biemiller advised the membership to face the fact that wage rates in Lancaster, Ohio, a rural community with no trade union tradition, in effect set sharp limits on Ray-O-Vac wage rates in Madison.[21]

Skaar resisted Biemiller's advice. Meanwhile, however, the WSFL representatives intensified their talks with the company. Apparently bypassing the local's Grievance Committee, Sigman's negotiations produced an agreement at the end of February. A harsh settlement, it called for a 15 percent wage reduction and pledged the union to vouch for the quality of the work performed. With little support from the local labor movement and with the icy blasts of the Wisconsin winter emphasizing their powerlessness, the battery workers approved it by a large majority.[22]

Although the 1939 settlement represented a setback, it did not immediately end the militants' influence. With Skaar as president and Lochner as chairman of the Grievance Committee, 19587 clung to its progressive political and trade union positions and to its stubborn bargaining posture throughout 1939. Its leadership continued to press the cause of the federal unions within the AFL, even as they explored contacts with CIO unionists locally and nationally. In Madison, the Grievance Committee closely scrutinized Ray-O-Vac's implementation of the wage provisions of the February agreement, and as early as May it lodged complaints with the company over methods of recalculating hourly wages and piece rates. Refuting the company's contention that it was the newness of the work being done in Madison that caused slender pay envelopes, Lochner lashed out at Ray-O-Vac. In June, he charged that the company had used the threat of closing down the plant as a means of beating down wages. "In addition to this," he asserted, "the Company, emboldened by a belief that the Union was demoralized, has adopted practices which are calculated to further disrupt the membership." Eventually, after months of protracted negotiations, Ray-O-Vac did agree to improvements in the wage scale and to back pay adjustments for production workers.[23]

These revisions in the 1939 contract, however, represented the last achievement of the militants. State AFL representatives cracked down on their CIO contacts and conducted much of the negotiations with management with little consultation with the Grievance Committee. Although Skaar and Lochner continued to enjoy considerable rank-and-file support, they felt that the AFL representatives were undermining their positions. Skaar in particular accused Sigman and Biemiller of red-baiting; he became increasingly convinced that company officials and AFL state representatives were colluding to dampen the ardor and militancy of 19587.[24] Feeling that they could no longer function in good conscience in a union so dominated by AFL bureaucrats, Skaar and Lochner left their jobs in December 1939.[25] Under their leadership, 19587 had been a leader in the battery council movement, a progressive political voice, and a sharp critic of the company. As the company and the battery workers began to gear up for the defense orders that increasingly dominated Ray-O-Vac's production, the union would have to accommodate itself to a more moderate local leadership, closer AFL supervision, and an emboldened management. It had flourished in the yeasty days of the 1930s, but now it had to adjust to the different demands of a country at war.

VI.
Battery Workers at War

World War II posed new challenges and new opportunities for the American labor movement. The discipline imposed by wartime production helped to undermine the feisty activism of the 1930s. At the same time, unions grew in membership through extension of the organizing launched in the thirties and through a variety of union security schemes. Industrial relations moved away from the overt confrontations of the Depression years toward more bureaucratized forms during the war.

At the shop level, however, the extraordinary burdens and pressures of wartime production frequently triggered vigorous grass-roots activism. Although American workers loyally supported the war effort and achieved tremendous feats of productivity, they were not willing to abandon their traditions of protest and insouciance. Wildcat strikes, short work stoppages, informal sit-downs, and other forms of on-the-job protest punctuated the war years. Burdened by unsettled family circumstances, difficult working and living conditions, and lagging wage rates, American workers resorted in the war years to the same devices that they had always employed, often in the face of the objections of their union leaders.[1]

Ray-O-Vac battery workers followed this pattern of loyalty, productivity, and stubborn defense of their rights. As large numbers of war workers crowded into the Madison plant, conditions deteriorated. The union, by now firmly established, reaped the benefit of large numbers of additional members. Ray-O-Vac workers willingly toiled overtime and tolerated substandard conditions of employment. At the same time, they kept a careful eye on their contract and vigorously asserted their demands for wage and benefit adjustments. While duly impressed with the importance of their work for the war effort, they were entirely willing to voice their grievances and to authorize strike action.

Paralleling their dual course of cooperation and protest vis-à-vis the company was the workers' attitude toward the union. There was no question as to their basic commitment to trade unionism. Still, the war years were unusually turbulent ones, even chaotic, in the local's internal history. While the conflict between militants and moderates abated with the departure of Skaar and Lochner, personal animosities, differences over negotiation strategy, and jurisdictional problems combined with the pressures of wartime factory work and social life to make the period from 1941 to 1945 a bitterly divisive time for 19587.

During the war, Ray-O-Vac's Madison plant switched almost entirely to defense production. By 1943, over 90 percent of its output of batteries and related items went directly to the United States Army Signal Corps. Employment mushroomed, rising from around 500 production employees in 1939 to more than 1,500 by early 1943 and nearly 2,000 toward the end of the war. As Madison's young men went off to war, the labor force became increasingly female; by 1945 over 70 percent of production employees were women.[2]

Ray-O-Vac production workers during the war, as before, were largely unskilled or semiskilled. Battery production in Madison called for more than one hundred distinct operations. "There are employees engaged in mixing the ingredients that go into the core of the cells . . . , operators of core tamping machines, operators on the assembly line . . . , operators who seal cells . . . , operators who solder cross-connections and terminals, cell and battery testers . . . , operators who put the batteries into cartons and pack them into cases," noted a company job-description form. "Most of the work," this report declared, "is not heavy work but is work that requires dexterity." Another survey of Ray-O-Vac's operations revealed in the workers' own words the nature of the tasks typically performed. Lucile Hubbard dipped papers in asphalt for placement on the tops of batteries. Thelma De Gregory soldered sockets and loose wires, while Esther Torteria inspected dry cells and used "a gas torch to flame them and an air hose to blow off all excess dust and dirt." Another operation entailed transferring approximately 24,000 cells a day from a punching operation to a capping machine. The influx of new workers and the urgent demands for increased production robbed the plant of some of the familiar camaraderie of earlier days and underscored the burdensome, routinized character of much of the work performed in the battery plant.[3]

Fatter pay envelopes only partially compensated for the difficulties of wartime work. Throughout World War II industrial wages in general lagged behind price increases. The Little Steel formula of 1942 pegged wage increases to an assumption of modest inflation, but as early as 1943 workers around the nation had grown resentful over the deep inroads that the cost of living was in fact making on their relatively stable wages. The average industrial worker, if he or she did not achieve an upgraded job classification or considerable overtime work, lost ground in buying power during the war.[4]

Ray-O-Vac's workers followed these patterns. Wage rates recovered somewhat in 1940 and 1941 from the 1939 cutback, but basic structures changed little during the war. Many of the new war workers, of course, began employment at relatively low wage and skill levels. Moreover, the increasing percentages of female labor further depressed the wage structure, since the company typically observed at least a 20 percent wage differential between male and female labor, a situation that unionization had done little to change. Expansion of operations and the siphoning off of some experienced workers into the armed forces, of course, created opportunities for promotions and hence for higher pay through reclassification and upgraded skill levels. Moreover, the Madison plant's expanded work force could not meet Signal Corps needs in a normal work week and the battery workers eventually toiled a fifty-four-hour week, with time and a half for the overtime. Still, the economic benefits of World War II, insofar as the battery workers were concerned, derived largely from regularity of employment and these temporary opportunities for upgrading and extra income, not from intrinsic improvements in their basic circumstances.[5]

Even this relative prosperity exacted a toll. Facilities were crowded and inadequate. Accident rates soared. The large numbers of new workers created a degree of anonymity and impersonality hitherto not present. Even the company's efforts to brighten spirits evoked criticism at times. On one occasion some thirty-seven production employees signed a petition calling on the Grievance Committee to "ask the management to buy an entire new collection of Records to replace the old ones, which everyone is tired of listening to." Some parts of the plant were plagued with alternating periods of overheating and frigid drafts of outside air. With annoying frequency the pitch pile caught fire and sent employees straggling from nearby work areas to escape the acrid, pervasive fumes. What with these inconveniences, pressures, and hazards, the incessant repetition of even the most popular tunes must indeed have tried the patience of the overworked battery makers.[6]

The war years had important consequences for the union also. The local became increasingly dependent upon the AFL for leadership and advice. Its members paid little attention to political and social issues as it underwent serious internal instability. While the existence of the union itself was never in question and while membership rolls reached record figures, a group of machinists moved toward the formation of an IAM lodge. This development, together with personal conflicts and other obscure quarrels related perhaps to the rapidly changing composition of the work force, led to a series of chaotic meetings, periodic exchanges of personal insults, and frequent and sweeping changes in the local's leadership.

The growing influence of state AFL functionaries in the affairs of 19587 predated the war. David Sigman and Andrew Biemiller had played decisive roles in settling the 1938–39 lockout and had closely monitored the pro-CIO tendencies that cropped up. During the war, collective bargaining became a tripartite labor-management-government matter as never before. Although local men and women sought changes in the contract and at times seriously contemplated strike action, the key importance of Ray-O-Vac's product in the military effort ensured that essential matters of controversy would be mediated among the three elements at the upper echelons and would not be fought out on the picket line. Sigman and later WSFL Representatives Charles Heymanns and Patrick Rogers assumed the major burden of negotiations and bargaining, for these men with their national perspectives, access to AFL expertise, and contacts in government were presumably better able than 19587's fluctuating local leadership to thread the way through the bureaucratic maze that characterized wartime labor relations. Of course, many members of the federal union continued to criticize the AFL servicing of these directly affiliated bodies, feeling that the federation's functionaries were too preoccupied with legislative matters and too solicitous of the strong national unions to fight aggressively for the small federal unions. Many, however, were satisfied with Sigman, Heymanns, and Rogers, and during the war, efforts to increase the autonomy and influence of the federal unions virtually stopped, with meetings of Wisconsin federal unions consisting of little more than good fellowship and routine resolution passing.[7]

Turbulent conditions within the local also encouraged AFL officials to expand their role. The departure of Skaar and Lochner by no means ended the internal conflicts, although after they left the union's controversies appeared to have little ideological content. As early as 1939, elections of officers became closely contested and even disputed. Three ballots were required to determine the president in that year. Between December 1943 and December 1945, no fewer than four men held the presidency, with at least one resigning under fire. Membership on the Grievance Committee also shifted frequently. In January 1940, the members of the union adopted a motion "that the president appoint four or five sarg. at arms to help keep order at . . . meetings." Two years later they adopted a motion "to stop dissension and false propaganda in [the] union." For several days in February 1941, Biemiller met with 19587's Executive Board seeking to restore order and "to straighten out internal dissension" arising from factional conflicts.

In 1945, charges circulated that some union members were criticizing the local's leaders in clandestine meetings with Ray-O-Vac officials, while other rumors held that the local's president was using union funds for beer parties. Sigman, Biemiller, Heymanns, and other AFL representatives repeatedly warned 19587 to stop its backbiting and quarreling. Finally, in December 1945, Frank Fenton, AFL director of organization, threatened the local with a disciplinary receivership. "The union," wrote its secretary in a paraphrase of Fenton's warning, "would be watched very close by the AFL regional office. Unless the discontentment stopped they would take this local over."[8]

Several factors contributed to this chronic internecine conflict. The great expansion of the labor force, the problems of civilian life in a scarcity-prone economy, the departure of some trusted leaders to military service, and the generally unsettled and trying working conditions no doubt played their parts. In addition, many workers found the practice of unionism unusually frustrating during the war, since so many matters formerly subject to legitimate dispute were now beyond the pale.[9] The breaking away of a group of skilled machinists to form Badger

Lodge 1406, IAM, in 1945 concluded a long and bitter quarrel. Some machinists had felt thwarted by being in the same bargaining unit as unskilled production workers, while battery workers resented this display of disunity and elitism. Moreover, the AFL increasingly encouraged federal unions to accede to craft encroachments or to be taken over in toto by the appropriate national union. Still further unsettling matters for 19587 was the fact that between 1939 and 1943 its president and other officers were machinists, who later became charter members of Badger Lodge 1406.[10]

In addition to wartime tensions and jurisdictional problems, much of the conflict within the local was purely personal. In December 1943, Paul Hein was elected president, only to resign nine months later amid charges that he sought domination over the Grievance Committee. Some members suspected fellow workers of being too friendly with management and of making de facto collective bargaining arrangements with company officials outside the negotiating structure. In August 1945, a former president of 19587 active in the IAM Lodge, accused the incumbent president of the federal union of personal use of union funds.[11]

Whatever the sources of discontent and antagonism, they had little to do with ideology or even militancy. Aside from the jurisdictional dispute over the machinists, 19587's members seemed to quarrel in part because the field for legitimate confrontation with management was so greatly narrowed by the contingencies of war and by the dominance of AFL officials. With membership growing—thanks to union security arrangements—the union was frustrated in its desires to do the things that unions were designed to do. The members of 19587, cut off from the heady combination of militant bargaining and trade union activism of the prewar years, fell to attacking each other over the shreds of prestige and limited emoluments available.[12]

This sense of frustration and powerlessness was revealed in the pattern of collective bargaining that developed during the war. Since output at the Madison factory consisted largely of high-priority items for the Signal Corps, neither the AFL officials nor government labor experts were content to leave matters to company management and the union, for both sides had proved stubborn and headstrong in the past. Ray-O-Vac's unionists were compelled to defer key demands and to watch as their fate was decided by government agencies and cumbersome bureaucratic processes.

For the union, collective bargaining became a kind of shadowboxing. Its position was frustrating in that the war years swelled membership rolls and created a demand for industrial labor in the area, a unique circumstance in Madison. With a strong union and a tight labor market, 19587 could normally have expected to redress the historically low wages at Ray-O-Vac. In 1940 and 1941, union contracts did gain wage concessions, but these did little more than balance the reductions forced in 1939. Throughout the war, local unionists sought to reopen the basic contract and make improvements in wages, vacation provisions, seniority, and other matters. Before American entry into the war, the company and the union engaged in a confusing round of disputes in which Ray-O-Vac unilaterally announced a wage increase, possibly after the urging of some moderate unionists who felt the company's generosity would help to mend the bitterness of 1938–39. Other unionists vigorously condemned Ray-O-Vac, however, arguing that the proffered increase was substantially lower than what company officials had verbally promised and that the method of granting it usurped the union's function. The affair culminated in a full-fledged dispute, with commissioners from the United States Conciliation Service entering the picture. In the end, union members received a small additional wage increase but many emerged from the affair further convinced of the company's duplicity.[13]

Bargaining during the war years proper proved even more frustrating. By December 1942, with union ranks augmented by new war production employees and with wages lagging behind prices under the Little Steel formula, resentment against the company burst forth again. Unionists felt that the time had come to redress the reductions embodied in the 1939 contract and to achieve other improvements in their basic working agreement, including better provisions regarding down time, seniority, regularity of the workday, and vacations. Unionists also sought strong arbitration provisions, hoping that this device might pry from the company concessions that its normally stubborn bargaining posture would not otherwise permit.[14]

With the contract up for renewal as of February 25, 1943, the Grievance Committee informed Ray-O-Vac on December 22, 1942, of its desire to seek changes. Company officials interpreted this to mean that the union desired the termination of the contract upon expiration, in which case, under a Wisconsin statute passed in 1939, the union would be required to obtain recertification for union shop purposes. For the next four months the company bargained on specific issues only reluctantly, contending that until the legality of the union shop—to which it claimed it had no objection per se—was decided, it could not sign a binding contract. Unionists felt strongly that the union shop issue was a bogus one, designed to tie up the union in legalistic maneuvering and to erode the solidarity and enthusiasm displayed by the membership in its demands for contract improvements.[15]

Early in February, the two parties reached an impasse in their direct negotiations. Because of Ray-O-Vac's importance in war work, U.S. Conciliation Commissioner James B. Holmes was quickly dispatched to Madison. According to his report the battery workers were convinced that the company was using the union's adherence as an AFL affiliate to the no-strike pledge as a means of avoiding substantive collective bargaining. The union, Holmes was convinced, felt it "absolutely essential to change [the existing] contract."[16]

Company officials reiterated to Holmes their unwillingness to contemplate contract changes until the legal issue of the union shop was decided. Vice-president Leroy Berigan repeatedly stated that the company was entirely satisfied with the contract originally negotiated in 1939 and slightly amended in 1940 and 1941. He felt that the wartime emergency was no time to contemplate substantial revisions in the document, arguing that wage rates were entirely adequate and that existing rules governing down time, seniority, and hours of operation had to remain exclusively within the company's control because of the seasonal and sporadic demand for its products. Ray-O-Vac especially opposed any efforts to introduce permanent arbitration provisions, contending that over the years the union and management had settled all disputes and grievances amicably through direct discussions. The introduction of third parties, company spokesmen argued, would disrupt what had been a harmonious and efficacious pattern of labor relations.[17]

Faced with such obduracy and emboldened by its restive membership, the union stood poised to strike. Holmes worked to achieve an interim agreement while negotiations continued. On February 18, he thought he had reached a tentative settlement, wherein the old contract would continue while both sides reviewed their bargaining positions. The company, however, took Holmes' effort to mean that the union had agreed to extend the contract for another year without change. At this point Holmes recommended certification of the case to the National War Labor Board.[18]

Company officials professed to dislike the interjection of federal agencies into the bargaining process, but they used the resultant bureaucratization of collective bargaining effectively. On one hand, company officials felt that the union would have been content with the old contract and would not have made demands that Ray-O-Vac deemed extravagant "if there were no Board from which the union thought it might obtain something without having the responsibility of reaching an agreement." On the other hand, company officials repeatedly insisted on punctilious observance of bureaucratic details, often to the annoyance of the federal representatives assigned to the case. Thus, Harry Malcolm, NWLB special representative assigned to effect mediation, met with both parties in late March 1943. After the March 26 meeting, he was convinced that a basis for settlement of the union shop issue had been laid and that in the interim collective bargaining on substantive contract proposals would proceed. But at the next meeting on April 7, company representatives arrived with new proposals concerning the union shop problem and adamantly resisted every union bargaining demand. Thus, observed Malcolm, "The Company's action in reviving the all-union shop issue and their [negative] attitude towards arbitration" and other contract issues seemed to wipe out all previous progress. Furthermore, the company insisted that its own very narrow concessions on bargaining issues would have to be accepted by the union without change. All of this, Malcolm felt, substantiated statements made by company officials during previous negotiations "that the Company preferred to operate without a Labor Contract of any kind."[19]

Eventually, the National War Labor Board's Region VI headquarters in Chicago named a tripartite panel to hear arguments on the case. Union and management representatives filed briefs and on April 22 appeared at a hearing in Madison. The panel eventually agreed with the union's contention that the union shop issue should never have been allowed to interfere with the collective bargaining process and issued an order, under powers granted by presidential proclamation, to maintain union shop status. Meanwhile, the panel, according to its chairman Meyer Kastenbaum, "put considerable pressure on both parties to attempt to reach an agreement by negotiation."[20]

By now, the union found its bargaining position eroded. Eager for a showdown around the turn of the year, its energies had been dissipated in legal and bureaucratic maneuvering. The Grievance Committee had started out by demanding substantial changes in the contract but had had to devote much of its attention to the company's oblique attack on the union shop. Bound by the no-strike pledge and by the unwillingness of AFL representatives to encourage bold militancy, and under great pressure from federal authorities for patriotic reasons to reach a settlement, the Grievance Committee abandoned many of its demands. The contract eventually signed on May 3 and ratified by the membership shortly after represented little improvement over previous documents. The company's concessions were largely temporary. Improvements were made in seniority and down time arangements, but the company insisted on a provision that reaffirmed its ultimate control over all work assignments, thus blunting the force of these gains. The union abandoned its demand for a 10 percent wage increase, while the company agreed to incorporate the current wage rates, which were in effect higher than those negotiated in 1941, in the contract. But even this modest concession was to prevail only during the war, with union and management to renegotiate wage rates upon the termination of the conflict. The Grievance Committee succeeded in having Ray-O-Vac agree to submit irresolvable differences to NWLB arbitration, but the contract pointedly specified that these third-party arrangements were wartime expedients only. In short, although its membership was large, its place in the labor market uncommonly favorable, and its product in great demand, Federal Labor Union 19587 was largely unable to take advantage of its position of temporary strength. As usual, the company bargained hard and skillfully used the very bureaucratic processes it condemned to blunt the union's militant thrust and to ensure that changes in the contract and in the pattern of labor relations would be minimal.[21]

Throughout the war, neither party professed to like the regimentation and bureaucratization of collective bargaining that resort to the NWLB occasioned. Unionists felt frustrated, unable to use their unusually strong position to improve basic contractual provisions. Moreover, local officers were forced to rely on AFL representatives, because governmental processes involved briefs and other paper work far beyond what the unpaid local officers were able to prepare in their spare time. For its part, Ray-O-Vac resented the intrusion of federal authorities, feeling that the presence of third parties constituted an undesirable precedent and finding them overly sympathetic to labor's point of view. In outrage over an NWLB hearing officer's findings on a 1945 job classification case, Leroy Berigan accused the official of believing that "American labor needs to be coddled to the point where publicly appointed officials must call black white in order to make cases come out labor's way." Still, just as federal involvement in labor relations had been instrumental in the birth of Federal Labor Union 19587 and had been an important factor, through the efforts of the Conciliation Service, in establishing a pattern of regular bargaining, the National War Labor Board also served its purpose. Although unionists were frustrated and resentful and the company chafed at interference, Ray-O-Vac employees kept on the job. turning out batteries and related products uninterrupted throughout the conflict.[22]

Thus, during World War II Madison battery workers made significant contributions to the war effort. At the same time, they kept a sharp eye out for their own interests. Although the wildcat strikes and periodic slowdowns and job actions that affected other war factories did not occur on a large scale at Ray-O-Vac, the battery workers were keenly aware of the inconveniences and lagging wage rates that accompanied the war. Their militancy succumbed to the increasing dominance of AFL officials, eager to cooperate with governmental efforts to step up wartime production. They were frustrated by a company management that wanted to ensure the preservation of existing arrangements, and they were stymied by the bureaucratization of industrial relations to which the war gave birth. Partly because of these abnormalities, 19587's members turned upon each other and the union leadership in a series of nasty upheavals and internal conflicts.

Still, by the end of the war, the local's status was even more firmly assured. Whatever else had been accomplished, 19587 survived internal conflict as it had survived earlier company harassment. The National War Labor Board reaffirmed its union shop in 1943, and it seemed unlikely that the company, although disturbed over the problems that might arise in dealing with two distinct unions after the creation of the IAM lodge in 1945, would really want a confrontation. If the battery workers were a disputatious lot, prone to internal bickering, they had always rallied around the union when its existence was threatened. Now with the war over and the likelihood of government wage restrictions being eased, the union could turn away from its internal conflicts and begin to improve its members' standards. Thus, some thought it an augury of future progress when at its December 1945 meeting the membership overwhelmingly chose the sober, responsible, widely respected Max Onsager as president over the controversial incumbent, Frank Bidgood.[23] After the sacrifices of the war years, 19587's members hoped that they had put aside turbulence and contention and could resume the progress in a brighter postwar world.

FLU 19587 and the
Postwar Era

Tranquility and steady progress were not in store for 19587 in the immediate postwar years. At a March 1946 meeting amid spirited discussion of the local's impending contract negotiations, members warned of the dangers of innuendo and rumor. "The disrespectful murmurings and literature adorning lavatory walls and behind persons' backs," declared one speaker, threatened to continue the bitterness of recent years.[1]

The union faced real challenges. Contract negotiations with a management determined to hold the line clouded the collective bargaining picture at Ray-O-Vac. In addition, Skaar returned to production work and to an active part in union affairs. His angry militancy and his determination to link 19587 to progressive forces in the labor movement found ready support, especially among younger workers and returning servicemen. Meanwhile, the inexorable process by which federal unions, often without conscious effort on the part of AFL staff people, lost their vitality and slipped into the embrace of large national unions was beginning. Thus, if the unique circumstances of the war had shaped the growth and development of 19587, equally unusual circumstances in the postwar American milieu posed other, no less difficult, challenges.

The American labor movement as a whole emerged from World War II enormously strengthened both in numbers and in prestige. Many observers saw the months immediately following the conflict as a crucial testing time for the unions. Radicals and liberals hoped that the labor movement, with its enormous gains in organization, could play a pivotal role in emerging liberal politics. Business executives and conservative leaders feared that the unions, having achieved and consolidated a strength never before enjoyed by the American labor movement, would move toward an increasingly socialized economic order. The great new industrial unions would not only provide the political muscle for expanded health, welfare, and social service legislation; they would attempt to gain entry into the sanctuaries of corporate board rooms and records files, claiming a major voice in hitherto private decision making. Many unanswered questions faced the labor movement as it emerged from the war. Would it lead a third party or push the Democratic party irrevocably leftward? Could it be relied upon in the developing confrontation with communism? Would it continue the gains it had been making for nearly fifteen years, or were there natural limits to trade unionism's appeal to American workers? Would the unions demand and receive an expanding role in the actual conduct of the American economic system, or could the changes of the '30s and '40s be codified into a stable system of bureaucratized collective bargaining? These were vital questions for the men and women of Federal Labor Union 19587, as well as for millions of other American workers.

Massive industrial conflict afflicted the country during the latter part of 1945 and the first half of 1946. Strikes by auto, meatpacking, steel, electrical, and communications workers, together with walkouts by coal miners, railwaymen, and thousands of additional workers in virtually every industry rocked the nation. These large-scale work stoppages were crucial in several respects. The UAW strike against General Motors, for example, raised forcefully the question of union access to company records and thus whether unions which had won their spurs in the 1930s would be able to take the next step — participation in corporate decision making — in the 1940s. The industrial conflict of 1945–46 brought to a head the question of the ability of the unions, born in the unique circumstances of the 1930s and 1940s, to survive and prosper in postwar America. Union members, pinched by inflation and hurt by sharp cutbacks in production accompanying the war's end, seethed with militancy and demanded quick results. A public and Congress equally fearful of inflation, fed for years with antilabor propaganda, and increasingly hypnotized by the specter of communism, seemed eager to chasten the restless laborites. The Truman administration responded to the syndrome of inflation, public concern, and labor unrest with a combination of uncertainty and repression. The election of an ardently conservative Congress in 1946 increased the flow of legislative proposals designed to weaken organized labor. The postwar period was indeed a testing time for the unions.[2]

The years immediately following the war posed particularly difficult problems for the labor movement in Wisconsin. As an industrial state, of course, it suffered the wave of strikes afflicting the rest of the country. In addition, the Wisconsin legislature, after a period of sympathy for organized labor in the mid-1930s, grew increasingly conservative and, in the words of the Madison-based *Union Labor News,* administered a "terrible beating" to organized labor "because public enemies got in control." Nationally, Wisconsin contributed newly elected Joseph R. McCarthy to the Republican-controlled Eightieth Congress.[3]

Wisconsin also harbored some of the most bitter conflicts between the AFL and the CIO, antagonisms that erupted in full force after the end of the war. Militant CIO unions such as the steel workers and auto workers contained large blocs of industrial workers in the Badger State and CIO leaders hoped in the postwar months to extend organization by challenging AFL control of city central bodies and by raiding AFL unions. The state CIO's left-wing reputation and the charges of communist influence that often surrounded it strengthened the resolve of AFL leaders to bolster their existing organizations and to carry the fight to their opponents. Throughout the late 1940s, WSFL and AFL Regional Office organizers scurried about the state, reinforcing city centrals, carefully servicing and propagandizing their federal unions — obvious targets of the industrially minded CIO's attentions — and fighting to maintain supremacy.[4]

These broad national and state controversies directly affected the restless and frustrated members of FLU 19587. They demanded substantial wage increases and other improvements in their contract immediately after the war. William Skaar returned to union affairs in 1946, first as a vocal rank-and-filer, later as president. Under his leadership, the union fought vigorously for collective bargaining gains, renewed its interest in social and political issues, and resumed its efforts to strengthen the position of the battery workers and the federal labor unions within the AFL. It was during this period too that Skaar and other militants, unhappy over the caution and conservatism of the AFL establishment, renewed contacts with CIO unionists, possibly contemplating eventual departure from the AFL and affiliation with a union such as the UE.

Of the many problems remaining between workers and

management, none was more important to the union member than the handling of grievances. Neither the initial contracts dating back to the mid-1930s, nor those signed during the abnormal conditions of the war years, had established an effective grievance processing system. In 1947, the Grievance Committee observed that production workers faced indirect, but very real, retaliation from supervisors if they dared file grievances. Workers frequently complained about misunderstandings of piece rates, job assignments, seniority rankings, and similar matters.

Often employees' complaints were more personal — protests against arrogant and insulting treatment at the hands of supervisors and against the impersonality of life in the factory. "Is it to be understood that Noral Hart [a foreman] will be allowed to use profanity while talking to employees?" inquired three aggrieved production workers one day in 1948. In April of the same year, Richard Michaels filed a grievance over losing his job because he talked to the girl working next to him. "It's the next thing to impossible to stand, and work next to a person all day long without speaking to them," he insisted.[5]

The grievance handling system that emerged over the years combined shop-level activism, personal contact, and AFL bureaucracy. Workers in the various departments elected their shop stewards. Just as rank-and-file members of the union alternated between the militant and moderate factions at the plant level, so workers of both dispositions were frequently chosen as grievancemen and grievancewomen. Some were aggressive champions of the ordinary worker in the classic mold of the fighting shop representative; others stressed conciliation, understanding, and personal contact with foremen and managers. There were times when an aggressive steward shut down the line until company representatives rectified glaring inequities. At other times, a quiet word or two to an angry foreman or discontented worker constituted the grievance system. Over the years selection of stewards was determined less by a worker's reputation for militancy or caution than by the problem of finding people willing to serve in these difficult positions.[6]

AFL influence tended to bureaucratize grievance procedures and to stress the need for accommodation and conciliation. The federation frequently stressed to employers that unionization would improve shop discipline and efficiency; 1958[7]'s contracts often contained extensive statements defining the responsibility of the union and its members for the quality of product.[7] Moreover, in a federal labor union, local grievance-persons were weakened by the fact that ultimate sanctions and support for their actions rested less on their fellow workers than on the judgment of AFL representatives. Aggressive stewards could shut down lines, but they could not be sure that AFL representatives operating out of Milwaukee would back them. They might persuade the local membership of the necessity for the action only to find crucial backing absent if the AFL withheld strike sanction or otherwise refused support. Since AFL staff members had many duties in addition to servicing the federal unions, they were anxious to work out regular, step-by-step processes and to remove matters as far as possible from both the militant shop-level enthusiast and the ignorant or callous fore-man. Hence, AFL representatives emphasized cooperation and consultation between themselves and top management. The AFL was not insensitive to the grievances of the battery workers. At times, such as in the 1936 showdown, federation representa-tives backed McCutchin, Skaar, and the angry membership. Still, Sigman, the AFL man who provided most of 19587's representation in the late 1930s, was acting more in line with federation policy when in late 1939 he arranged with Ray-O-Vac's personnel manager for "a meeting between the shop stewards and foremen for the purpose of improving the rela-tionship between the management . . . and . . . the union."[8]

Still, the company resisted repeated union efforts to intro-duce outside fact-finding and arbitration processes for settling controversies. Throughout 1949, for example, AFL and WSFL representatives visited Madison on many occasions, seeking settlement of grievances involving disciplinary action against fifty-six employees and resolution of disagreements over new piece rates. The "company representative," observed Regional Director Friedrick, "adamantly refused to consider [the] griev-ance[s] and stated they would refuse to arbitrate."[9]

In addition to these festering problems over grievances, the company and the union bargained antagonistically and aggres-sively over wages and working conditions after the war. Un-ionists called in 1946, 1947, and 1948 for substantial wage increases, upwards of 20 percent, in addition to improvements in vacation provisions, down time, and seniority rights. They were convinced that the company could afford contract im-provements. An AFL Research Service Report for 1944 declared, "Net profit after all charges returned 25.4% on net worth . . . , an exceptionally good return on the capital employed in the business." A report prepared by the CIO United Electrical, Radio and Machine Workers was even more sanguine, stating that net profits had risen steadily from about $225,000 in 1939 to over $950,000 in 1946, with a projection of around $1,200,000 for 1948. Observed an envious fellow unionist to Skaar, "It should be sheer pleasure sitting across the table from an outfit sitting on top of that kind of money."[10]

Company officials resisted these initiatives. They pointed out that as early as the latter months of 1945 declining orders had resulted in considerable layoffs. Moreover, they contended that large wage increases in the contract to be negotiated early in 1946 would necessitate price increases, which in turn would require approval from the Office of Price Administration (OPA). Company officials were further convinced that the general atmosphere of the late 1940s called for restraint and sacrifices. They argued that profit margins were too narrow, that taxes on business were confiscatory, and that productivity in recent years had failed to keep pace with costs. If unionists saw the postwar era as a time in which to make important gains, management was equally determined to increase productivity and to restrain wages.[11]

It surprised no one that 1946 negotiations were bitter and protracted. Talks began in December 1945, but as of the expiration date of the existing contract, February 24, 1946, no agreement was near. The Grievance Committee, together with AFL representatives, continued to meet with company officers under periodic thirty-day extensions of the contract.

Both AFL representatives and the United States Conciliation Service commissioner assigned to the case were eager for their own reasons to arrange a quick settlement, but found Ray-O-Vac rigid in its bargaining posture. Friedrick accused the company of using delay tactics when it claimed that it could not negotiate meaningfully on wages until it had received OPA approval for price increases. Friedrick noted that other Madison firms had already granted considerable wage boosts and that one of Ray-O-Vac's chief competitors had recently signed a contract agreeing to a fifteen-cent raise. Yet in April, after four months of negotiations, the company proposed but a ten-cent increase, coupled with rejection of changes in other features of the contract.

Early in the year, union leaders had complained of poor attendance at meetings, but as the confrontation with management deepened, workers began to show up. At the March 20 meeting the local rejected a company proposal of eight cents. At the same time, the members filed a thirty-day strike notice as required by the Smith-Connally Act and asked Green for AFL strike sanction. The members buzzed with strike talk, with some unionists fearful of a step they had never before taken and others eager for action. Soon, however, both the apprehensive and the enthusiastic learned from WSFL Representative Charles Heymanns that, due to government and AFL procedures, it would be sixty days before they "walked the cement."

Friedrick urged Green to approve strike sanction, declaring, "if we do not get a strike sanction . . . I am afraid we will have a very bad situation in this union which may lead to its disintegration." Green eventually gave his approval. Conferences involving the local leadership, AFL representatives, company officials, and a USCS commissioner were held repeatedly throughout March and April. Even though Skaar and other militants were not at the time officers of the union, they constantly pressed both union and Ray-O-Vac officers and stood ready to rally the membership in opposition to a contract that granted too little. They led in the rejection of the company's March 19 offer and again in the defeat of a de facto ten-cent increase offer on April 22. Finally, on May 4, the local formally endorsed a strike vote against Ray-O-Vac by a thumping 535 to 16 majority. The battery workers, however, did not in fact join the national wave of strikes in 1946. Perhaps prodded by the workers' show of solidarity and determination, the parties returned to the bargaining table and emerged on May 9 with a fifteen-cent settlement, which the membership approved by a vote of 443 to 64.[12]

Relations remained strained in subsequent years. In 1947, the union again asked for an hourly increase of twenty cents, arguing that for years Ray-O-Vac had maintained standards below national patterns. The *Union Labor News* attacked the "disgracefully low base scale of wages . . . 68 cents per hour for women and 84 cents for men." It reported that "during negotiations the company admitted that the financial condition of the firm was very good, but maintained that this fact had no bearing on wage rates." Nor would the company consider serious revision of its rather minimal seniority, vacation, and fringe benefit standards.[13]

AFL and WSFL organizers sent to help 19587's bargaining committee grew perplexed and irritated with the company. It refused, for example, to revise arbitrary and eccentric vacation provisions that penalized workers laid off after accumulating putative vacation time. Friedrick complained in 1947 about the company's "peculiar position" not to renew the union shop provision of the agreement unless the workers agreed to drastic revisions in seniority rules. Again, during the 1948 negotiations, Heymanns grew exasperated with the company. Despite what appeared to be substantial profits and despite a recent union shop reaffirmation by an overwhelming majority of workers, Ray-O-Vac remained "stubborn and unrealistic."[14] The union served strike notice in both 1947 and 1948, as the company remained adamant in its resistance to basic improvements in the contract. By May 1948, both union representatives and USCS representatives felt that further conferences were "futile" and that a strike was almost certain.

But, as in 1946 and 1947, no strike took place. Increasingly aware of their vulnerability to wage competition in other battery centers and of the lack of employment in Madison, the Ray-O-Vac workers eventually accepted a disappointing increase of five cents an hour for 1948. Evelyn Gotzion, one of the most vigorous and knowledgeable members of the union, recalls the mixture of contempt and dismay with which the workers received these contracts. She carefully folded hers up and put it safely away, hoping that one day she would find it a source of bittersweet nostalgia in the light of what she hoped would be substantial improvements in the future. But for the time being at least, the company could indulge its hard bargaining reputation, and the workers, though belligerent, accepted what most considered to be inadequate settlements. The company's threats to move and lack of coordination among battery workers nationally once again undermined the bargaining posture of FLU 19587.[15]

Both AFL leaders and 19587's officers grasped the importance of these factors and sought to deal with them. By now, Ray-O-Vac was expanding its operations and could even more effectively threaten to move out of the Wisconsin capital in favor of locales with more tractable labor. With little alternative employment available, Ray-O-Vac workers had little choice other than to accept company offers, despite their outbursts of militancy. Increasingly to Skaar and other members of 19587 the lessons of postwar negotiations were clear: battery workers everywhere needed a cohesive organization, one that could move toward companywide collective bargaining and indus-trywide consultation. Without greater regional and national coordination, militant leadership, rank-and-file activism, and AFL strike sanctions would remain as futile as they had been in 1946, 1947, and 1948.

Unfortunately, throughout the late 1940s, the battery in-dustry remained an organizational jungle. With an industry prone to relatively small, decentralized production facilities anyhow, a variety of forms and degrees of organization had emerged over the years. At least six plants had been organized in the 1930s and 1940s, but no cohesive national body had formed. By the late 1940s, representation in battery factories was split among several unions. At the Ray-O-Vac facility in Wil-liamsport, Pennsylvania, for example, the UE (CIO) had or-ganized the workers, but after the union's officers refused to sign the anticommunist affidavit required by the Taft-Hartley Act for NLRB certification, a strike erupted, complicated by bitter rivalry between UE and AFL supporters. In 1948, a federal labor union won bargaining rights there, but conflict between AFL affiliates, both federal and international unions, and CIO bodies raged in other battery cities. In all, significant organizational activities in the industry were undertaken in the late 1940s by the UE, the UAW-CIO, the UAW-AFL, and the IBEW, an AFL craft union, as well as through federal unions.[16]

The attitude of AFL officials was ambivalent. On the one hand, for years the Executive Council had been discouraging the federal unions and resisting their efforts to form a cohesive bloc within the AFL. In addition, leaders in the dominant national unions disliked the prospect of a battery workers' union as a separate entity, both because the emergence of another industrial union would weaken craft control of the federation and because the IBEW and other extant unions already claimed jurisdiction. Ideally, AFL leaders would have preferred the rapid absorption of battery workers' unions into the IBEW, the UAW-AFL, or the IAM.

At the same time, local circumstances coupled with the CIO challenge did not permit this solution. Around the country, even cautious and moderate battery workers resented the effort to weaken their federal unions and to incorporate them into

AFL craft unions. Industrial versus craft unionism was no longer a radical-conservative issue, if it ever had been, for conservative unionists had no more desire than did militants to become second-class appendages to some scornful craft union. Nor did they wish to see a membership that had fought many battles together parceled out among several separate unions. At Ray-O-Vac in Madison, Max Onsager, a faithful AFL man and far from a militant on most issues, forcefully argued this view. Onsager, reported 19587's secretary, "emphasized the importance of Federal Labor Unions as opposed to craft unions. He pointed out how the crafts took the machinists from our union and how this would continue further by organizing our carpenters, line workers, etc. into separate craft unions and sap our strength still further." Moreover, federal unionists feared that even if their locals were incorporated as a bloc into craft unions they would be thought of as inferiors and treated as such. "The more people we have in one camp the greater our economic strength," observed Onsager, in words befitting a CIO militant. With such sentiments widespread, the AFL would clearly risk alienating even its strongest supporters in local unions if it pressed its anti-FLU campaign too vigorously.[17]

Shortly after the war, faced with the CIO challenge together with the commitment of many local unionists to maintain their FLUs, the AFL agreed to hold regular battery conference meetings. It undertook this action reluctantly because the creation of the conference delayed the absorption of local federal unions into appropriate national bodies and because the action might encourage those who envisaged a national industrial battery workers' union. Still, the AFL faced challenges from CIO unions and felt a need to give AFL battery workers support in their confrontations with battery companies lest AFL loyalists lose ground in CIO assaults. Hoping to guarantee that the Battery Workers' Conference (BWC) would not replicate the experiences of the industrial workers' councils that had emerged in the 1930s only to form the nuclei of key CIO unions, Green appointed Friedrick as chairman. From the viewpoint of William Skaar, who as president of 19587 was an active participant in the BWC, the conference represented a first, tentative step toward a full-fledged battery workers' union, one that could back the militant demands of locals with concerted action while at the same time exercising a progressive influence within the AFL. To the AFL establishment, however, the BWC represented a stop-gap measure. To be sure, it would aid locals in their negotiations with battery companies. Its long-range purpose, however, was to counter the CIO and eventually to ease the transition from federal union status to absorption by existing national unions.[18]

In line with AFL intentions, the BWC functioned as an information exchange rather than as the focal point of militant action. Its activities were limited largely to correspondence from Friedrick to the locals informing them of affairs in sister plants. The battery workers did gather several times a year under close AFL supervision to discuss common problems and to consider coordination of bargaining activities, but usually the conferences consisted largely of advice and reports from AFL officials. At the December 1948 meeting, Ray-O-Vac locals held a separate caucus and approved a motion by Skaar to have the BWC press for common contract expiration dates in the company's several facilities. Uniform contract expirations would have been a step toward companywide bargaining and hence a partial answer to 19587's perennial problem of management threats to relocate operations, but Ray-O-Vac consistently resisted this initiative and held out against companywide negotiations. Little took place at the battery workers' conferences to convince the company that it faced an aggressive mass organization that could successfully insist on this proposal; nor did the conferences otherwise encourage those in the unions who looked toward a militant industrial union of battery workers. Firmly controlled by AFL representatives, the BWC stood little chance of accomplishing the concerted action that militants had envisaged.[19]

In addition to their involvement with the Battery Workers' Conference, AFL officials attempted to persuade management to cooperate in the rationalization of collective bargaining in the industry. The unsettled situation at Williamsport had repercussions in other Ray-O-Vac facilities. In August 1948, D. W. Tyrell, Ray-O-Vac president, asked Friedrick for help in scotching rumors about union busting in Williamsport. Friedrick used this and subsequent opportunities to press on Tyrell the virtues of standard, companywide negotiations. Such negotiations, Friedrick agreed, would help the workers by establishing common contract expiration dates and help the company by reducing friction and controversy among workers in its several plants. Of course, standardized negotiations would also benefit the

AFL in its effort to keep CIO unions out of the industry. In April 1949, Harry E. O'Reilly, AFL director of organization, journeyed to Madison along with Friedrick to confer with Tyrell "on proposals to improve [the] bargaining procedure for all Ray-O-Vac plants organized under [the] A.F.L." Little came of this meeting or of similar ones to follow. Though Ray-O-Vac executives preferred AFL to CIO representation, there seemed little danger of massive defection to the latter organization, especially since its union in the electrical industry — the UE — was under heavy assault because of alleged communist influence and because its leaders refused to sign Taft-Hartley anticommunist affidavits. Moreover, battery workers themselves sometimes showed little concern for standardized negotiations. In December 1949, members of FLU 23529 at Ray-O-Vac's Sioux City, Iowa, facility agreed to extend their present contract through February 1951, despite Friedrick's advice that "such action would unfavorably affect negotiations at other Ray-O-Vac plants." Able to divide and dominate, management had little incentive to embrace companywide bargaining.[20]

Thus, efforts to coordinate collective bargaining and to develop some consistent pattern of trade unionism in the battery industry failed. With the AFL in no mood to sponsor new international industrial unions and with organization split between so many craft, federal, and CIO unions, negotiations in the battery trade remained uncoordinated and haphazard. Although representatives from WSFL and AFL Regional Offices and FLU 19587 spent much time and effort traveling to such places as Dubuque, Sioux City, Williamsport, Lancaster, and Paducah for organizational purposes and for conference meetings, in the final analysis the future of the battery workers lay with one or another of the industrial or craft-cum-industrial unions in the electrical or machinery trades. A cohesive organization of battery workers was impossible. If they resisted rapid absorption, their only hope of retaining strong, autonomous local unions with a stronger, more effective organization, lay in the creation of a separate, powerful department for federal unions within the AFL and WSFL.[21]

Members of FLU 19587 had always participated enthusiastically in efforts to organize and coordinate the battery industry. They also consistently supported moves to improve the status of the federal unions, both in the state and in the AFL generally. Ever since the surge of organization that followed the passage of the NIRA in 1933, the federal unions had been both promise and threat to the AFL. At the same time, federal unionists, dissatisfied with their second-class status in the federation, had periodically risen to protest and to assert their claims as the vanguard of the AFL's response to the need for industrial organization. In 1934, FLU representatives appealed to the AFL Executive Council to recognize their integrity and to treat them as permanent industrial organizations, immune from the jurisdictional forays of the crafts. At the 1937 convention, Skaar was among a group of federal unionists seeking similar aims. Again in 1947, 1948, and 1949, workers in these directly affiliated bodies attempted to assert themselves.

None of these efforts succeeded. The natural and institutional skepticism of the FLUs harbored by the AFL and craft union hierarchy was reinforced by the fact that groups of federal labor unions formed the core of such rebel organizations as the UAW and the United Rubber Workers. Even in the late 1930s, when membership in directly affiliated unions stood at more than 200,000 and FLU dues represented about 40 percent of AFL income, constitutional provisions kept them impotent. The original conception of the FLUs as mere holding bodies was reaffirmed, especially with the ascendancy of Secretary-Treasurer George Meany in federation affairs. The AFL clearly intended that the work of organization and collective bargaining was best carried on through the national unions, enabling the AFL itself to concentrate on such functions as political action, lobbying, research and education, public relations, and, increasingly, participation in the struggle against international communism.[22]

Still, the dream of a strong FLU presence within the AFL died hard. To progressive unionists, the directly affiliated unions stood as bastions of industrial unionism in the craft-ridden federation. To many moderate local unionists, the FLUs provided refuge from the foreign world of bureaucracy, political involvement, and dictation by arrogant business agents associated with the craft unions. Thus, Wisconsin's federal unions maintained a state FLU conference throughout the war years. Its meetings and functions, however, were routine, and it rarely raised basic questions about the status and future of the local organizations.[23]

After the war Wisconsin's federal unionists resurrected the idea of a vigorous FLU presence within the WSFL and the AFL.

Resentful over the decision of WSFL President George Haberman to dismiss the state's only federal union organizer, Rudolph Faupl, and convinced that the craft unionists who dominated WSFL politics held them in contempt, federal unionists asserted themselves. In mid-1946, the state's federal unions chose a steering committee to lead the drive for greater influence. "Our unification," declared the committee's secretary, "will prevent craft unions from cutting us up." For the next dozen years or so, regular conferences of state federal unions were held four times a year, under the auspices and tutelage of WSFL officials. Most conferences consisted largely of speeches by state labor and political leaders and workshops on such topics as labor law and bargaining techniques. But WSFL officers clashed with FLU activists, especially during the early postwar meetings, warning them against holding secret meetings and departing from the official agenda. Meanwhile the federal union delegates chafed under the restrictive hand of the state labor establishment.[24]

State federal union activists had two primary objectives aside from information exchange and discussion of common problems. In the words of their 1952 statement of purposes, they sought "to assist in stopping any raids upon the memberships of Federal Labor Unions by international unions both within and without the American Federation of Labor." They pledged "to continue all efforts to bring about a national organization or department of Federal Labor Unions." In regard to the first objective, the federal unions saw themselves as legitimate repositories of industrial unionism. While admitting that "the federal labor unions were born of necessity" and that at the outset they were "a minor segment of a major organization," FLU activists declared that they had achieved "a loose form of permanence." Workers, asserted a FLU manifesto of 1948, were loyal to the AFL, but they resented "being broken up and disrupted into smaller units" by the predatory craft unions. Over 200,000 workers belonged to federal labor unions, which were clearly their "choice of organization, and it is still after many years their choice to remain intact."[25] Through the years, federal unionists had found AFL officials reasonably sympathetic and often learned that the federation staff was favorably disposed toward them.[26] But the real governing body of the federation, the Executive Council, was controlled by the craft unions. With the favorably disposed Green in his dotage and the craft unions aggressively organizing mass production workers and gathering up thousands of federal unionists, the Wisconsinites grew increasingly apprehensive. "The situation has become worse within the past few years," wrote Gregory Wallig, as chairman of the State FLU Conference, to Green in January 1952. Protesting against raids by international unions, Wallig asserted that AFL representatives were using the "McCarthy brand of character assassination . . . against . . . local union leaders." Green's reply piously condemned such raiding of federal unions, but by 1952 their decline had become inevitable. Throughout the 1950s, and especially after the merger of the AFL and CIO in 1955, FLU membership in the state plummeted, falling from around 25,000 in their postwar heyday to under 16,000 in 1957.[27]

Federal unionists failed also in their efforts to influence the AFL to establish a separate department for directly affiliated unions in the federation. Wisconsin's grass-roots FLU activism established in the 1930s continued after the war; into the early 1950s the federal unions in the state constituted nearly 20 percent of AFL membership in Wisconsin. Large locals composed of farm implement, furniture, metal fabrication, and machinery workers in Milwaukee and Kenosha helped the federal unions to exert important influence in WSFL affairs. A 1947 AFL convention resolution noted that "in the state of Wisconsin there remains the largest group of federal labor unions in the United States." Throughout the 1940s Wisconsinites consistently represented between 20 and 30 percent of the FLU vote at national conventions.

Thus, it was natural that Wisconsinites should emerge as national leaders in the federal unions' fight for survival. In 1947, Wisconsin's federal unionists sponsored a resolution calling for sweeping changes in the AFL constitution to permit unrestricted organizing activities and to allow FLU representatives to submit resolutions directly to the national convention. Though the two delegates that the Wisconsin Federal Labor Union Conference sent to San Francisco in 1947 to observe proceedings returned with an optimistic report, the resolution was shunted to the federation bureaucracy for study and recommendation.

Again in 1949, the Wisconsinites sponsored a resolution calling for "a permanent national organization of federal labor unions" so that workers in directly affiliated bodies could exert cohesive influence within the AFL and develop their own organizing campaigns, train their own representatives, and choose their own national leaders. Both resolutions called for conferences between AFL officers and FLU representatives — "presumably from Wisconsin," read the 1947 proposal — to work out means of strengthening the FLUs.[28]

Members of 19587 actively supported these activities. Onsager, Skaar, and others regularly attended state FLU conference meetings. They continually sought to educate the local membership about the grievances of the FLUs and pledged themselves to continue to battle against "'taxation without representation.'" The local consistently contributed funds to promote FLU activities and send representatives to AFL conventions to present the views of the federal unionists.[29]

These efforts of the late 1940s, however, were no more successful than similar moves in previous years. At the 1937 AFL convention, FLU activists had fought vigorously, only to have the convention put them off with a bland motion to have the Executive Council investigate the advisability of establishing an AFL-FLU liaison body. In 1948, the Executive Council once again dismissed the FLUs' appeals, rejecting a proposal to create a separate FLU department and promising only to investigate further the status of the directly affiliated unions. The FLUs' 1949 resolution declared, "The time has come for the American Federation of Labor of recognize the permanence that has been achieved by the federal labor unions." The convention once again responded with a vague recommendation that AFL officers and organizers continue their efforts to help the directly affiliated unions.[30]

Far from increasing their influence, federal unionists saw their impact on the AFL decline with each passing year. With the CIO challenge abating and with the AFL ever more firmly committed to the dissolution of the FLUs, local unionists found themselves ever more firmly controlled by AFL representatives while they received less and less adequate service from these officials. Skaar for one understood this. He maintained contacts throughout the late 1940s with UE activists and with Wisconsin CIO people. On several occasions he vocally criticized the AFL for allegedly collaborating with management in Ray-O-Vac factories elsewhere to undermine UE organizing activities. As president of FLU 19587, Skaar longed for association with the broader, more militant, and, to him, more effective unionism that these organizations stood for.[31]

Skaar was never able to move the local in this direction. As in the 1930s, it was clear that, while the membership would vote him into office and follow his aggressive bargaining line up to a point, there was little overall interest in the kinds of risks and commitments that departure from the AFL would entail. Skaar was convinced that AFL officials would use any excuse to expel him anyway, given his dissident role in union affairs over the years. If he so much as hinted at UE affiliation, he felt sure that AFL officials, no doubt backed by the influential moderate faction in the union, would stop at nothing to discredit him. Much later he remarked that, given his conception of what a union should be together with the circumstances that in fact determined 19587's course, during those years in the union he was living a kind of lie.[32]

In May 1949, FLU 19587 celebrated its fifteenth anniversary. In many respects, the results of a decade and a half in the labor movement were modest. Workers at Ray-O-Vac remained relatively poorly paid, while the company's decentralization of operations and adoption of labor-saving machinery reduced the work force at the Madison plant. The company remained a tough collective bargaining opponent. True, grievance procedures, seniority, and other benefits won by the union had reduced some of the fear and insecurity, but as late as November 1947, the union's Grievance Committee still complained of arbitrary and intimidating treatment of workers. "It is with regret," protested Onsager, "that we must admit that some of our employees hesitate and even refuse to sign grievances for fear of retaliation from their supervisors."[33]

The place of the union in the labor movement as a whole was another problem. With organized labor in general stuck on dead center, preoccupied with its internal quarrels and absorbed in Cold War concerns, Skaar and other militants were perennially disappointed by the AFL's caution and by their own inability to arouse positive enthusiasm for political action and identification with the more progressive forces in the labor movement. More moderate activists, while fully content with AFL affiliation, grew increasingly resentful over the declining status of the federal unions and ever more apprehensive over the likelihood of fragmentation or absorption by the crafts.

Still, few Ray-O-Vac workers wished to abandon the union. On August 1, 1946, 511 production workers of 636 eligible voted in a representation election, with 19587 receiving 500 positive ballots. Again in March 1948, production workers endorsed the union shop by a vote of 587 to 10.[34] Clearly, whatever the workers' disappointments in collective bargaining gains and in their assessment of their place in the labor movement, 19587 had established itself as a permanent and necessary part of the working lives of Ray-O-Vac employees. Over the years, the union had undergone many battles — some with the AFL, others among the members. There were losses and gains, victories and defeats, but through it all there were few in the union who would dispute Skaar's view that 19587 was "one of the most interesting and active federal labor unions."[35]

Epilogue

In April 1963, Federal Labor Union 19587 closed its books and became United Automobile Workers Local 1329.[1] The departure of the UAW from the AFL-CIO in 1968 severed its last direct connection with the parent AFL. Today, Ray-O-Vac is part of a conglomerate, ESB Industries. With diversified investments, decentralized manufacturing, and increasing reliance on overseas labor and automation, the company's work force in Madison has steadily dwindled. As of January 1975, there were about 175 union production workers, and even as I talked with the local's current officers and early activists, rumors of further cutbacks circulated.

Just as in its formative years, Ray-O-Vac in its more recent history has both replicated and stood apart from broader tendencies in the labor movement. Certainly, the decline of blue-collar employment in central cities is part of a national pattern, as in the replacement of English, German, and Scandinavian workers with members of ethnic minorities. Abandoning the federal union to affiliate with an international organization followed a long-time AFL (and later AFL-CIO) policy. With UAW affiliation, too, came a greater commitment to political action as an integral part of the union's activities, a development very much in line with trends in the labor movement as a whole.

In important respects, however, the battery workers have not conformed to the overall patterns. In general, most observers of the labor movement would characterize the decades of the 1950s and 1960s as years lacking in militancy and laborite activism. While it is true that in the 1950s the battery workers chose relatively conservative local leadership, it is also true that they walked the picket line for the first time in 1956. Strikes lasting several months also occurred immediately after UAW affiliation in 1963 and again in 1968. Thus, while the battery workers avoided strikes in such tempestuous years as 1934, 1936–37, and 1946, they pounded the pavement regularly in the presumably prosperous and quiescent years of the 1950s and 1960s.

Affiliation with the UAW and their subsequent departure from the AFL-CIO also went against the stream. For years, AFL officials had sought to steer 19587's members into a national union, preferably the International Association of Machinists or the International Brotherhood of Electrical Workers. By the 1950s, the federal unions born in the 1930s were being rapidly phased out; since 1940, the AFL had issued few new federal charters, and the AFL-CIO merger in 1955 further discouraged this form of organization. Yet, state AFL officials had always worried about the freewheeling militancy that periodically surfaced in 19587 and no doubt preferred that one of the more cautious national unions absorb the federal union. Certainly, they had no desire to see a long-term AFL affiliate link up with the auto workers, a CIO union with a long record of dissidence and aggressiveness in Wisconsin.

For their part, 19587's activists were divided over the desirability of abandoning the federal charter. To Max Onsager and to Mrs. Lawrence Grab, who became president in 1956, absorption by a large national union would make the Ray-O-Vac workers but cogs in a large machine. They felt that a national union would involve local workers in remote political controversies and that its representatives could not understand or respond to the unique problems of the company and the workers in Madison. In particular, they regarded the UAW with suspicion, given its liberal commitments and its reputation for social involvement. When it became apparent by the end of the 1950s that the AFL-CIO was determined to end federal status, some of 19587's most loyal and dedicated veterans seriously contemplated going independent and thus severing all connections with organized labor rather than accept affiliation with a national union.

In light of AFL preferences and the vigorous opposition of these long time and respected leaders, the choice of the UAW ran counter to the prevailing tendencies. Although by 1960 the auto workers' union had lost some of its reputation for crusading militancy, it still stood clearly to the left of the AFL-CIO establishment. Affiliation with the UAW with its broad program of labor education, its espousal of liberal social policies, and its strong commitment to political action, represented a kind of victory — long delayed, to be sure — for the sort of trade unionism that William Skaar and other militants had fruitlessly advocated for so many years. Thus, in the heady days of militant unionism, Ray-O-Vac battery workers made do with the relatively cautious and dependent status of a federal labor union, while the somnolent era of the fifties and sixties saw them embrace at least an attenuated form of the broad laborite activism that they had avoided in the past.

There has been a labor union now at Ray-O-Vac for more than forty years. At the time of its establishment, it represented a conjunction of production workers with little knowledge of trade unionism and the proud American Federation of Labor. The union has survived many challenges. It faced sharp opposition from management in the 1930s and 1940s. It experienced frustrations and difficulties at the hands of the AFL bureaucracy. It endured the irritations of wartime labor relations only to be plunged into the confusion of the turbulent postwar labor scene. It has undergone bitter internal conflicts, and its members have at various times espoused sharply divergent notions about the nature and purposes of trade unionism. They have suffered through lockouts, waged strikes, and fought repeatedly with management, the AFL, and each other.

It is impossible to assess the overall impact of the existence of Federal Labor Union 19587. Company officials repeatedly declared that the union's unrealistic demands forced them to automate and to develop cheaper production operations elsewhere, thus draining the city of jobs. Unionists hotly contend that it was only through the union that battery workers were able to gain a modicum of job security, along with better wages, paid vacations, and other benefits.

In the final analysis, though, trade unions take on significance less from the final line of the balance sheet than from their status as the unique and exclusive institutions of working people. It has been through FLU 19587 and its successor UAW Local 1329, created and maintained by the workers themselves, that Madison battery workers have sought to come to grips with significant aspects of their working lives.

Notes

I. THE BATTERY WORKERS AND AMERICAN LABOR HISTORY

1. Recent textbook literature illustrates this point. William E. Leuchtenberg, general editor, *The Unfinished Century: America since 1900* (Boston: Little, Brown, 1973) and Paul K. Conkin and David Burner, *A History of Recent America* (New York: Crowell, 1974), for example, contain only the most marginal comments about organized labor in their respective treatments of the period since 1946. Lawrence S. Wittner, *Cold War America: From Hiroshima to Watergate* (New York: Praeger, 1974) devotes considerably more attention but is unrelentingly critical. Equally instructive are recent essays by New Deal scholars James T. Patterson and Otis L. Graham, Jr. Both are concerned with the broad impact of New Deal era reforms on the course of American history to the present. Neither contains more than a passing reference to the labor movement. James T. Patterson, "American Politics: The Bursts of Reform, 1930s-1970s," in Patterson, ed., *Paths to the Present: Interpretive Essays on American History since 1930* (Minneapolis: Burgess, 1975), pp. 57–101, and Otis L. Graham, Jr., "The Planning Ideal and American Reality: The 1930s," in Stanley Elkins and Eric McKitrick, eds., *The Hofstadter Aegis: A Memorial* (New York: Alfred A. Knopf, 1974), pp. 257–99, esp. pp. 284–89.

The assumptions contained in this paragraph are obviously debatable. For support, see Andrew Levison, *The Working Class Majority* (New York: Coward, McCann, and Geogehegan, 1974); Brendan Sexton and Patricia Cayo Sexton, *Blue Collars and Hard Hats: The Working Class and the Future of American Politics* (New York: Random House, 1971); Irving Howe, ed., *The World of the Blue Collar Worker* (Chicago: Quadrangle, 1972), and, especially, Michael Harrington, *Socialism* (New York: Saturday Review Press, 1972), chs. 6 and 11.

Critics abound. Intelligent, conservative criticism of the unions has atrophied of late, but see Terry Catchpole, *How to Cope with COPE* (New Rochelle, N.Y.: Arlington House, 1968). The left has been far more interesting. See, e.g., Jeremy Brecher, *Strike!* (San Francisco: Straight Arrow Books, 1972); Stanley Aronowitz, *False Promises: The Shaping of American Working-class Consciousness* (New York: McGraw Hill, 1973); and editors of *root and branch, Root and Branch: The Rise of the Workers' Movements* (Greenwich, Conn.: Fawcett World, 1975).

2. Actually, labor music of this sort was a cultural hybrid, as synthetic as it was exuberant. See R. Serge Denisoff, *Great Day Coming: Folk Music and the American Left* (Baltimore: Penguin, 1973), esp. pp. 70–98.

3. The disaffection of many liberals, fixated on the contrast between the heroic past and the mundane present, also plagues organized labor. For recent journalistic commentary along this line, see, e.g., Haynes Johnson and Nick Kotz, *The Unions, Washington Post National Reports* (New York: Bantam Books, 1972), and William Serrin, *The Company and the Union: The "Civilized Relationship" of the General Motors Corporation and the United Automobile Workers* (New York: Vintage Books, 1974).

4. The standard histories of the 1930s — the books by Irving Bernstein, Sidney Fine, and Walter Galenson, for example, cited in the Bibliographical Essay — contain much evidence of these kinds of tendencies, although likely none of those authors would agree with the emphasis put on them there. My article, "The Limits of Militancy: Organizing Paper Workers, 1933–1935," *Journal of American History* 63 (December 1976): 638–57, examines some of these themes in depth.

5. Donald Sofchalk, "The Little Steel Strike of 1937" (Ph.D. dissertation, Ohio State University, 1961), pp. 152–54; George Douglas Blackwood, "The United Automobile Workers of America, 1935–1951" (Ph.D. dissertation, University of Chicago, 1951), pp. 154–58; Morris Janowitz, "Black Legions on the March," in Daniel Aaron, ed., *America in Crisis: Fourteen Crucial Episodes in American History* (New York: Alfred A. Knopf, 1952), pp. 305–25; Gary Trade Marx, *The Social Basis of the Support of a Depression Era Extremist: Father Coughlin* (Berkeley: Survey Research Center, University of California, 1962), pp. 112–15. See also Robert S. Lynd and Helen Merrell Lynd, *Middletown in Transition: A Study in Cultural Conflicts* (New York: Harcourt Brace, 1937), pp. 41–42, 463, 508, and Caroline Bird, *The Invisible Scar* (New York: David McKay, 1966), pp. 191–93.

6. See, e.g., J. David Greenstone, *Labor in American Politics* (New York: Alfred A. Knopf, 1969), esp. pp. 52–58; Penn Kemble, "Rediscovering American Labor," *Commentary* 51, no. 4 (April 1971): 45–52. On the sitdowns, see Sidney Fine, *Sit-Down! The General Motors Strike of 1936-1937* (Ann Arbor: University of Michigan Press, 1969), p. 174. See also David Brody, "Radical Labor History and Rank-and-File Militancy," *Labor History* 16, no. 1 (Winter 1975): 117–26.

II. BEFORE THE UNION

1. John W. Alexander, *An Economic Base Study of Madison, Wisconsin* (Madison: University of Wisconsin, School of Commerce, Bureau of Research and Service, June 1953), pp. 16, 31–32, 34–35, 69–70, 76, 81,

84; *The French Flasher* (Employees' Association newspaper), November 1919; *Ray-O-Lite News* (same publication, title changed periodically), October 1923 and November 1923; *Ray-O-Vac Sparks,* March 1956.

2. Alexander, *Economic Base Study;* Edgar Z. Palmer, *The Prewar Industrial Pattern of Wisconsin,* Wisconsin Commerce Studies (Madison: University of Wisconsin, 1947), pp. 11–12, 96–97, 123; Calvert Lampert Dedrick, "Incomes and Occupations in Madison, Wisconsin" (Ph.D. dissertation, University of Wisconsin, 1933), pp. 6, 30, 32; James Paul Collins, "Real Property and Low Income Area Survey of Madison, Wisconsin" (M.A. thesis, University of Wisconsin, 1941), pp. 5, 6, 10–14, 17, 105–10; Daniel Herschel Kruger, "A Study of Collective Bargaining in Wisconsin" (Ph.D. dissertation, University of Wisconsin, 1954), pp. 45–46, 179.

3. There was a small but lively local of the American Federation of Teachers at the University in the 1930s (Local 223). Its members included such prominent labor scholars as Don Lescohier, Elizabeth Brandeis, and William Chalmers. Literary critic and biographer Mark Schorer served as its secretary. Its records are housed at the State Historical Society of Wisconsin in Madison (SHSW). In addition, the American Federation of State, County and Municipal Employees originated in Madison in 1932 and had its headquarters there for many years. Gregory Wallig, a veteran Wisconsin unionist, commented on the relative lack of industry and on the resultant anomalism of industrial unionism in Madison in my interview with him. (The interviews conducted for this study and the dates on which they took place are listed in the Bibliographical Essay at the end of this book.)

4. Richard Skinner Allis, "Urban Redevelopment Study of a Selected Area in Madison, Wisconsin" (M.S. thesis, University of Wisconsin, 1947), pp. 12–15, 17; Collins, "Real Property," pp. 5–6, 12–14, 105–10; Gerald Lochner radio transcript, "Workers' Education Program," November 17, 1939, Papers of Federal Labor Union 19587, SHSW, Box 3 (hereinafter cited as FLU 19587 Papers); *Union Label News* (Madison), November 1939, p. 4. The title of this publication changed to *Union Labor News* in 1942.

5. There are many references to addresses and visits to the local union by University of Wisconsin faculty and students scattered through FLU 19587's records. For the Ely-Commons-Perlman tradition, see Paul James McNulty, "Economics and the Study of Labor" (Ph.D. dissertation, Cornell University, 1965), esp. p. 230. Selig Perlman's student David Saposs was a close observer of the federal labor unions. See Folder 8/10, Box 8, David Saposs Papers, SHSW, and Saposs, "Industrial Unionism," *Journal of Political Economy* 43, no. 1 (February 1935): 69–83.

6. Alexander, *Economic Base Study,* pp. 34–35.

7. Robert Nesbit, *Wisconsin: A History* (Madison: University of Wisconsin Press, 1973), pp. 460–61; Collins, "Real Property," p. 12; interview with Pat Lowe.

8. Leo Wolman and Gustav Peck, "Labor Groups in the Social Structure," in Research Committee on Social Trends, *Recent Social Trends in the United States: Report of the President's Research Committee on Social Trends* (New York: McGraw-Hill, 1933), vol. 1, p. 845. The best introduction to welfare capitalism in the 1920s is in Irving Bernstein, *The Lean Years: A History of the American Worker, 1920–1933* (Boston: Houghton Mifflin, 1960), pp. 144–89. Stuart Dean Brandes, "Welfarism in American Industry" (Ph.D. dissertation, University of Wisconsin, 1970), pp. 236–58, describes the kinds of activities characteristic of Ray-O-Vac's welfare program. See also Robert H. Zieger, "Herbert Hoover, the Wage-earner, and the 'New Economic System,'" to be published in *Business History Review* (Summer 1977), for additional citations and observations.

9. *French Flasher*, July 1919.

10. E.g., ibid., November 1919.

11. Hubbard's observations are extolled in ibid.; the quote is in the August–September 1920 issue.

12. Ibid., April 1925 and May 1926.

13. For one of the few comments on social issues, see the editorial "Workers Oppose Radicals," ibid., October 1927. L. G. Berigan's rose-colored view of the factory appears in his "Berripickins" column in the January 1920 issue.

14. Ray-O-Vac's reputation for low wages and the prevalence of other problems were frequently alluded to in interviews with union veterans. E.g., interviews with Evelyn Gotzion, Pat Lowe, and Marion Shaw; and telephone interview with William Skaar. Interviews with David Sigman and Gregory Wallig revealed that this assessment of Ray-O-Vac was widely shared in labor circles through the state. See also Gerald Lochner, radio transcript, November 17, 1939, FLU 19587 Papers, Box 3.

III. STARTING THE UNION

1. These impressions of the ethnic and social background of Ray-O-Vac workers were gleaned from interviews conducted in January 1975. Surnames in the records of the union are almost without exception German, Scandinavian, and English. See also Collins, "Real Property," p. 17, and Kruger, "Collective Bargaining in Wisconsin," pp. 45–46, 179. In 1930, for example, Madison's foreign born constituted only 9.1 percent of the population, compared, for example, with Racine's 21.2 percent.

2. Interview with David Sigman; clippings in Wisconsin State Federation of Labor Papers, SHSW, Box 1. (Hereinafter cited as WSFL Papers.)

3. Interview with David Sigman; interview with Gregory Wallig; Harold J. Newton, "Profiles of Past and Present Labor Leaders — Henry Ohl, Jr. (1917–1940)," *Wisconsin Labor — Bicentennial Edition* (1975–76), p. 39; clippings, WSFL Papers, Box 1.

4. Marion Shaw particularly noted McCutchin's tireless efforts. *Ray-O-Lite News,* April 1925, carries a brief biography of him in recognition of his promotion to foreman. McCutchin's role and company harassment of him is revealed in a series of complaints, reports, letters, and rulings in Docket no. 241, National Labor Relations Board Records (RG 25), NLB 1933–34 and NLRB 1934–35 Regional Records, Region X (Chicago), Federal Records Center, Suitland, Md. The words quoted in this paragraph appear in Myrna Auringer to Joseph Vejlupek, January 17, 1935, FLU 19587 Papers, Box 1.

5. The best source for an explanation of the difficulties and high attrition rate of the federal labor unions is AFL Papers, Series 7, Strikes and Agreements File, American Federation of Labor Records, SHSW. (Hereinafter cited as AFL-Series 7.) For commentary, see Harry A. Millis and Royal Montgomery, *Organized Labor* (New York: McGraw-Hill, 1945), pp. 203–9, and James O. Morris, *Conflict within the AFL: A Study of Craft versus Industrial Unionism, 1901–1938* (Ithaca: New York State School of Industrial and Labor Relations, 1958), pp. 59–63, 146–47, 151–59. The words quoted in this paragraph are contained in David Saposs to Evans Clark, April 6, 1934, David J. Saposs Papers, SHSW, Box 3.

6. Most union veterans interviewed mentioned work force characteristics noted in this paragraph. Membership figures are contained in AFL report, May 4, 1936, AFL-Series 7, Box 27. Skepticism regarding the 80 percent figure is based on the fact that in 1935 there were about 700 production workers. Although no doubt organization grew between 1935 and 1937, there is no documented proof that the local had achieved such a high percentage, especially since the AFL based its calculations on monthly averages, always a lower figure than the most recent monthly report in a growing union. For some suggestive observations on the reasons for successful organization among rank-and-file workers, see E. Wight Bakke, "To Join or Not to Join," in Bakke, Clark Kerr, and Charles Anrod, eds., *Unions, Management, and the Public: Readings and Text,* 3d ed. (New York: Harcourt Brace, 1967), pp. 85–92.

7. Interview with Max Onsager.

8. Sol Reist to Carl Steffensen, acting secretary, Chicago Regional Labor Board, May 24, 1934, Docket 241, NLRB Records. Docket 241 contains the correspondence and rulings on this case, which resulted in William McCutchin's reinstatement without back pay.

9. H. E. Page to W. C. Holden, August 26, 1935, American Federation of Labor Papers, Series 4, Industry Reference Files, SHSW, Box 36. Interviews with William Skaar, Evelyn Gotzion, Byron Buchholz, David Sigman, and Gregory Wallig.

10. The pattern of caution and militancy became clear in conversations with almost all of the veteran unionists interviewed.

11. William McCutchin and Myrna Auringer to Whom It May Concern, August 31, 1934; same authors to W. W. Cargill, December 12, 1934; Auringer to Joseph F. Vejlupek, January 17, 1935, FLU 19587 Papers, Box 1.

12. Myrna Auringer to Donal Weber, August 14, 1935, ibid.; FLU 19587 Minute Books (hereinafter cited as MB), April 16–August 12, 1935; correspondence between L. G. Berigan and William McCutchin, March 22, April 1, April 17, and May 2, 1935, FLU 19587 Papers, Box 1; Auringer to William Green, May 28, 1935, Green to Auringer, June 4, 1935, Green to Sol Reist, June 4, 1935, Auringer to Green, June 16, 1935, Reist to Green, June 18, 1935, Green to Auringer, June 21, 1935, and Green to AFL Representative Paul Smith, June 21, 1935, AFL-Series 7.

13. Robert E. Mythen to Hugh Kerwin, October 2, 1935; Mythen Preliminary Report, September 18, 1935; "Agreement with Production Employees," dated October 1, 1935, all in United States Conciliation Service Records (RG 280), Federal Records Center, Suitland, Md., File 182-716 (hereinafter cited as USCS Records); MB, May 14–October 1, 1935, passim.

14. William McCutchin to William Green, April 8, 1936; W. W. Cargill to McCutchin and to William Skaar, April 9, 1936; Cargill to Employees of Ray-O-Vac, April 13, 1936, all in AFL-Series 7; statement of Cargill, ca. April 15, 1936, and letter from Robert E. Mythen to Hugh Kerwin, April 21, 1936, USCS Records, File 182-1388; MB, April 9–May 14, 1936, passim.

15. Transcripts of these meetings of April 8, 1936 — made without the approval of the workers involved — are in USCS Records, File 182-1388.

16. MB, April 13, 14, 1936; transcript of Skaar-Cargill conversation, April 8, 1936, USCS Records, File 182-1388; David Sigman to William Green, April 14, 1936, AFL-Series 7.

17. David Sigman to William Green, April 20, May 1, 5, 15, 1936, AFL-Series 7; MB, April 8–May 15, 1936; Robert E. Mythen to Hugh Kerwin, May 21, 1936, USCS Records, File 182–1388.

18. David Sigman to William Green, May 15, 1936, AFL-Series 7.

19. In view of its subsequent success and militancy over the next several years, there is no reason to doubt Sigman's judgments on the strengthening effect of the 1936 controversy, contained in ibid.

20. Ibid.

21. Unfortunately, FLU 19587's records, while unusually copious for a local union, do not contain a file of contracts. There is a model contract in ibid., but it contained suggested benefits far beyond those the company was willing to contemplate in 1936. Contracts for 1937, 1939, and the war years can be seen among the materials in Case No.

111-581-D, Selected Documents from Region VI Case Files, Records of the National War Labor Board (World War II) (Record Group 202), National Archives, Federal Records Center, Suitland, Maryland. The union's minute books, beginning with the entries for the summer of 1936, reflect the growing importance of the contract in the minds of union members. By 1938, it was the dominant feature of most meetings, as the membership sought improvements in the original union shop agreement of March 4, 1937. See, e.g., MB, November 10, 1936; July 23, 1937; May 31, June 24, 1938. Also, interview with Evelyn Gotzion.

22. Lochner radio transcript, November 17, 1939, FLU 19587 Papers, Box 3.

23. Interview with Evelyn Gotzion.

IV. The Battery Workers and the Labor Establishment

1. Interviews with David Sigman and Gregory Wallig.

2. Interview with David Sigman.

3. Interview with William Skaar.

4. Ibid.; interviews with Gregory Wallig and David Sigman. All of the members of 19587 interviewed had strong remembrances of Skaar.

5. Interview with David Sigman.

6. Interview with Max Onsager. The observations in this paragraph are a composite of the impressions gained from other interviewees from 19587 and from Gregory Wallig.

7. Interviews with David Sigman and Gregory Wallig. The papers of most federal labor unions operating in Wisconsin — 18456 (Simmons Furniture, Kenosha); 18545 (Kohler Company, Kohler); 19649 (aluminum workers, Two Rivers); 19641 (appliance workers, West Bend); 20070 (food processing workers, Whitewater); 19593 (Parker Pen, Janesville); 19806 (A. O. Smith Manufacturing Company, Milwaukee); 22631 (International Harvester, Milwaukee); and many others — are contained in AFL-Series 7. Wisconsin State Federation of Labor, *Proceedings of the Thirty-eighth Annual Convention, 1930* (Milwaukee, 1930), pp. 10–15; WSFL, *Proceedings of the Forty-third Annual Convention, 1935* (Milwaukee, 1935), pp. 11–20.

8. This section on the federal unions is based on the books by Morris and Millis and Montgomery (see ch. 3, n. 5) and Lewis L. Lorwin, *The American Federation of Labor: History, Policies, Prospects* (Washington, D.C.: Brookings Institution, 1933), pp. 70–72, 325–26, 327, 335, 363–64; Philip A. Taft, *The A.F. of L.: From the Death of Gompers to the Merger* (New York: Harper and Row, 1959), pp. 55–60, 96–97; and Estelle Stewart, *Handbook of American Trade Unions — 1936 Edition*, Bureau of Labor Statistics Bulletin No. 618 (Washington, D.C.: GPO, 1936), pp. 8–13. Constitutional provisions regulating the FLUs appear

at the beginning of the annual *Report of the Proceedings of the Annual AFL Convention*. Careful readers of these *Proceedings* can also trace in fragmentary fashion the largely futile efforts of the federal unionists to strengthen their position in the AFL. One such early effort, directed at the AFL Executive Council, occurred in January 1934 and is chronicled through documents in the Saposs Papers, Box 8, Folder 8/10. Finally, the hundreds of files in AFL-Series 7 contain a wealth of information on the FLUs.

9. Interviews with William Skaar, Gregory Wallig, and David Sigman; organizers' reports, WSFL Papers, Boxes 5–8; Joseph C. Goulden, *Meany* (New York: Atheneum, 1972), pp. 72–73.

10. Interview with David Sigman. Sigman's organizing activities and the esteem in which he was held can be seen in organizers' reports, WSFL Papers, Boxes 5–8, and in many communications in AFL-Series 7. E.g., Fern Garlock, secretary of FLU 20070, Whitewater, to William Green, February 9, 1937: "We wish to thank you for referring Mr. Sigman to us, for he has settled . . . important matters. . . . If it hadn't been for him our Union wouldn't have gained recognition."

11. Organizers' reports, WSFL Papers, Boxes 5–8; interviews with David Sigman and Gregory Wallig; Harold J. Newton, "Jake Friedrick . . . Mr. Union Leader," *Wisconsin Labor — Bicentennial Edition* (1975–76), pp. 27, 29, 31.

12. Interviews with Byron Buchholz and Gregory Wallig; organizers' reports, WSFL Papers, Boxes 5–8; Wallig memo, July 12, 1976, to author; Wallig, sketch of Charles Heymanns, *Sheboygan Labor Day Program*, 1973.

13. Interviews with Max Onsager and William Skaar.

14. Ibid. Visitors' and speakers' names are recorded in MB. On appreciation for AFL help, Myrna Auringer to William Green, May 19, 1936, AFL-Series 7, Box 27; Ruth E. Hippe to Green, August 12, 1941, ibid. On strike sanction, Green to David Sigman, May 6, 1936, ibid.

15. Interview with William Skaar; MB, August 6, 1935.

16. Examples of 19587 members' organizing activities can be seen in MB, March 5, June 25, August 12, August 20, 1935, April 30, October 13, November 26, 1937, February 22, March 11, 1938, and in Joseph F. Vejlupek to Myrna Auringer, January 20, 1936; Auringer to Mr. Priebe, August 6, 1936, Auringer to Vejlupek, September 14, 1936, and many other communications, 1935–39, in FLU 19587 Papers, Box 1. An AFL research report contained in H. E. Page to W. C. Holden, August 26, 1935, AFL Papers, Series 4, Industry Reference Files, Box 36, estimates the extent of organization in the dry cell battery industry.

17. Interview with William Skaar. Skaar to Antony Sadar, March 6, 1935, FLU 19587 Papers, Box 1; MB, November 18, December 6, 1938 (on battery council), July 22, October 7, 1938 (FLU council). The *Report of the Proceedings of the Fifty-seventh Annual Convention of the American Federation of Labor* (Washington, D.C., 1937) contains nothing on the

fight to strengthen the federal unions, suggesting that the federal unionists were unable even to gain a hearing. The local did lay out $248 for Skaar's trip to Denver (MB, September 3, 1937), and correspondence reveals that he did seek to join with other federal union representatives to further the FLUs' interests (Myrna Auringer to Walter Hohler, November 23, 1937, FLU 19587 Papers, Box 1).

18. The MFL's help can be traced in MB throughout 1934. Sol Reist, an MFL organizer, helped McCutchin in his appeal to the National Labor Board for reinstatement (Sol Reist to Carl Steffensen, acting secretary, Chicago Regional Labor Board, May 25, 1934, Docket no. 241, NLRB Records). The growing quarrel with the MFL can be seen in MB, April 16, 1935, February 4, April 21, 1936, January 8, 15, 1937, and in Myrna Auringer to MFL, November 5, 1936, FLU 19587 Papers, Box 1. See also *Union Labor News,* December 1945, p. 11.

19. On the city centrals, see Stewart, *Handbook,* p. 52, and Lorwin, *American Federation of Labor,* pp. 346–49. Lorwin points out, however, that since city centrals in the nineteenth century often surpassed the AFL and the national unions in influence, the federation was always fearful of overly encouraging them.

20. Interview with William Skaar; MB, April 16, December 10, 1935, February 4, August 11, November 5, 1936, January 8, June 11, 1937; motion of August 11, 1936, and Myrna Auringer to B. Dolnick, August 15, 1936, FLU 19587 Papers, Box 1; Paul Krakowski, "Press Treatment of Wisconsin Labor Issues, 1936–1938" (M.A. thesis, University of Wisconsin, 1947), pp. 31–32. Lochner's comments are in his letter to Albert A. Shanks, August 10, 1939, FLU 19587 Papers, Box 3.

21. Interview with William Skaar; motion of August 11, 1936, FLU 19587 Papers, Box 1. See MB citations, note 18 above, for 19587's sympathetic attitude toward the CIO.

22. MB, August 10, 11, 1936, June 11, 1937; Myrna Auringer to B. Dolnick, August 15, 1936, FLU Papers, Box 1; Krakowski, "Press Treatment," pp. 30–31.

23. Interview with William Skaar; MB, August 11, September 1, 1936. The early days of the still-militant UE are chronicled in James J. Matles and James Higgins, *Them and Us: Struggles of a Rank-and-File Union* (Englewood Cliffs, N.J.: Prentice-Hall, 1974), pp. 22–53.

24. Interview with William Skaar; interview with David Sigman; Sigman to Frank Fenton, June 13 and 20, 1939, AFL-Series 7.

V. TROUBLED TIMES, 1936–40

1. Wisconsinites played a significant role in the labor controversies of these years, but their story has yet to be adequately told. For impressions of the charged atmosphere and tempestuous events, see Nesbit, *Wisconsin,* pp. 523–25; Robert Willard Ozanne, "The Effects of

Communist Leadership on American Trade Unions" (Ph.D. dissertation, University of Wisconsin, 1954), part II; Walter H. Uphoff, *Kohler on Strike: Thirty Years of Conflict* (Boston: Beacon Press, 1966), pp. 35–102; and Thomas W. Gavett, *Development of the Labor Movement in Milwaukee* (Madison: University of Wisconsin Press, 1965), pp. 152–96.

2. For citations and commentary on these works, see the Bibliographical Essay at the end of this book.

3. Ozanne, "The Effects of Communist Leadership" deals with UAW Local 248, Allis-Chalmers, but it concentrates almost exclusively on the issue of communism. Three works do contain useful material on local unionism in this period. See John G. Kruchko, *The Birth of a Union Local: The History of UAW Local 674, Norwood, Ohio, 1933–1940* (Ithaca: New York State School of Industrial and Labor Relations, 1972), Peter J. Friedlander, *The Emergence of a UAW Local, 1936–1939: A Study in Class and Culture* (Pittsburgh: University of Pittsburgh Press, 1975), and Claude E. Hoffman, *Sit-Down in Anderson: UAW Local 663, Anderson, Indiana* (Detroit: Wayne State University Press, 1968). See also remarks in the Bibliographical Essay at the end of this book.

4. Actually, such terms as "faction," "militant," "conservative," and even "struggle for control" are somewhat misleading. FLU 19587 had no formal caucuses and apparently no tightly organized blocs or consistently articulated ideological dichotomies. Still, sharp differences did exist concerning the function of unionism and approaches to collective bargaining. Interviews with William Skaar and Max Onsager provided much of the material for this chapter.

5. The observations in this paragraph are based on a careful reading of the union's records and correspondence for the 1930s, together with the interviews conducted in January 1975. Cf. Robert Lynd and Helen Merrell Lynd, *Middletown in Transition: A Study in Cultural Conflicts* (New York: Harcourt Brace, 1937), pp. 41–43, 503, 509, for observations about the lack of visible indications of working-class solidarity in another middle western city in the thirties. Ray-O-Vac employees evinced a greater ability for self-organization and were less inclined to be attracted to reactionary hate groups than were Middletown's workers. See also Friedlander, *Emergence of a UAW Local,* pp. 111–31, and David Brody's review, *Reviews in American History* 4, no. 2 (June 1976): 266, for illuminating commentary on these themes.

6. The observations in this paragraph are drawn largely from MB, July 7, 1936, January 22 and 24, 1935.

7. These observations are based on the interviews conducted in January 1975 and June 1976. Cf. Brody's review of Friedlander, *The Emergence of a UAW Local,* in which he states, "Unionism was . . . a quite narrow band in the total experience of the modern American worker" (p. 266).

8. The interviews with Evelyn Gotzion and William Skaar suggested the political involvement of some members, while those with

Max Onsager and Mrs. Lawrence Grab revealed opposition to political activities. Typical political stands of this period are indicated in MB, September 3, 1937, January 7, 1938, March 11 and 18, 1938.

9. Union shop since 1937: Lochner radio transcript, November 17, 1939, FLU 19587 Papers, Box 3. Progressive political stands: MB, November 26, 1937, January 7, March 11, 18, 1938. Sympathy for CIO: MB, August 10, 11, 1936, June 11, 1937, February 18, 1938, and interview with William Skaar. The quotes in this paragraph are contained, respectively, in Myrna Auringer to Walter Hohler, November 23, 1937, and Harvey T. Riley to members of FLU 19587, November 4, 1937, FLU 19587 Papers, Box 1.

10. Interview with William Skaar. Evidence of grievance handling is almost nonexistent for this period, but Cargill's interview with Skaar during the 1936 controversy reveals the union activist to have been extremely articulate and independent. Certainly by the late 1930s many members of the union were convinced that management wanted to get rid of Skaar and Lochner for their allegedly intransigent, contentious attitudes (MB, December 13, 1938).

11. Interviews with Max Onsager and Mrs. Lawrence Grab; interview with Byron Buchholz; MB, January 6, February 3, 1939.

12. Interview with William Skaar; interview with Pat Lowe. Max Onsager emphasized that, while the company was a tough collective bargaining opponent, it had been his experience that its officers had been generally forthright and responsible. Onsager, who worked at Ray-O-Vac for over forty years, did not let his staunch loyalty to the union interfere with his pleasurable social relationships with company officials. See also MB, December 1938–February 1939.

13. Interviews with William Skaar and Max Onsager. Onsager stressed his view of the union as part of a system of harmonious industrial relations, a view that the AFL in general had urged on employers for years, particularly in the 1920s.

14. Skaar's interview depicted the rank and file as willing to contemplate militant and politically progressive programs but as having no deep, abiding commitment to this course. Onsager thought that it was a handful of firebrands, backed by some of the younger workers, who pressed this line. In the final analysis, it is difficult to tell exactly where the labor movement's tendency toward bureaucracy and caution shaped the responses of shop-level workers and where workers themselves directly asserted their felt interests. The fact, however, that 19587's militancy was most sharply voiced and tenaciously held concerning the most basic kinds of trade union demands — security for the union, seniority, wage increases — together with the overall impressions left in my mind from 19587's records and my interviews, lead me to conclusions about the relationship between militancy and bureaucracy, activism and apathy, similar to those suggested by David Brody. See the Bibliographical Essay at the end of this book for citations. See

also Warren R. Van Tine, *The Making of the Labor Bureaucrat: Union Leadership in the United States, 1870–1920* (Amherst: University of Massachusetts Press, 1973), pp. 85–112, for an illuminating examination of the theme of the relationship between union leadership and rank-and-file workers. Although Van Tine's study deals with an earlier period, his observations are pertinent to the activities of FLU 19587 in the 1930s and 1940s.

15. Ray-O-Vac statement and brief, ca. April 1943, Case No. 111-581-D, Selected Documents from Region VI Case Files, Records of the National War Labor Board (World War II) (Record Group 202), National Archives, Federal Records Center, Suitland, Maryland; MB, May 31, June 24, July 5, December 13, 16, 27, 1937; interviews with William Skaar, Max Onsager, and Pat Lowe.

16. MB, May 31, June 24, July 5, 1938.

17. MB, December 13, 16, 27, 1938; David Sigman to Lewis G. Hines, AFL director of organization, December 13, 1938, AFL-Series 7; interviews with William Skaar, Byron Buchholz, Pat Lowe, and Max Onsager.

18. Interview with Max Onsager. As early as 1935, unionists had acknowledged that although "our employer has never refused to bargain with us . . . our Employer thinks we are unfair to push him too far when there are other Battery concerns that are employing Non-Union help" (Myrna Auringer to Donal Weber, August 14, 1935, FLU 19587 Papers, Box 1). But by 1940, AFL organizers were making substantial efforts to extend organization of battery workers, especially when the threat of CIO activity arose (David Sigman, report dated week of December 2, 1940; Charles Heymanns, reports dated December 19–21, 1940, organizers' reports, WSFL Papers, Box 5).

19. Onsager and Lowe have vivid memories of what Onsager calls "the 1938 disaster" and the hardship it imposed. Internal conflict is revealed in MB, December 1938–February 1939. The words quoted are in the January 6, 1939, entry.

20. Skaar's resignation and election: MB, December 16, 1938; rejection of company offer and Skaar's opposition to Biemiller's advice: MB, January 20, 1939.

21. In his interview Onsager said he believed that the AFL initially followed an unrealistic "no backward step" attitude, only to reverse itself in light of the lockout. The role of Sigman and Biemiller is indicated in MB, January 20, Febuary 3, 1939, and in a series of letters from Sigman to Frank Fenton, who replaced Hines as AFL director of organization, February 7, 20, 27, March 15, 1939, AFL-Series 7.

22. Contract approval (by a vote of 355 to 13): MB, February 24, 1939. A copy of the agreement appears in Sigman to William Green, March 15, 1939, AFL-Series 7. See also *Union Label News,* March 1939, p. 2, and June 1939, p. 4.

23. In March, the union endorsed Lochner's candidacy for city

alderman (MB, March 17, 1939). The controversy with the company over implementation of the 1939 agreement can be traced in MB, June–November 1939. The same span illustrates the continuing popularity of Skaar and Lochner among the rank and file, at least if selection to represent the union at the state federation of labor convention is any indication. The fullest account of the controversy, and one that reveals the increasing influence of AFL representatives in 19587's affairs, occurs in a series of letters and copies of letters among Lochner, Sigman, Fenton, and Green, May 22, 1939–November 7, 1939, AFL-Series 7. Lochner's bitter words about the company's intentions are contained in his letter to Green, June 26, 1939, AFL-Series 7.

24. Interview with William Skaar.

25. Gerald Lochner to Louis Ufnowski, December 6, 1939, FLU 19587 Papers, Box 3; interview with William Skaar. For a time, they helped a run a co-operative grocery store on Madison's east side. In 1940, Skaar, whose sister Nora had married Selmer Rorge, a high-ranking Ray-O-Vac officer, became safety director of the company (Skaar to Ruth Hippe, July 5, 1940, FLU 19587 Papers, Box 3).

VI. BATTERY WORKERS AT WAR

1. The standard account is Joel Seidman, *American Labor from Defense to Reconversion* (Chicago: University of Chicago Press, 1953). See also Nelson Nauen Lichtenstein, "Industrial Unionism under the No-strike Pledge: A Study of the CIO during the Second World War" (Ph.D. dissertation, University of California, Berkeley, 1974); Joseph C. Goulden, *Meany* (New York: Atheneum, 1972), ch. 5; Jeremy Brecher, *Strike!* (San Francisco: Straight Arrow Books, 1972), pp. 221–31.

2. Alexander, *Economic Base Study*, pp. 16, 35, 70; Situation summary, August 14, 1941, USCS Records, File 196-6124; James B. Holmes, USCS Commissioner, Preliminary Report, February 19, 1943, ibid., File 300-2594; Holmes, Final Report, March 2, 1945, ibid., File 455-0601.

3. A number of employees' handwritten job descriptions appear in FLU 19587 Papers, Box 6, Folder for December 1945–January 1946; company brief, n.d., but ca. April 1943, Case No. 111-581-D, Selected Documents from Region VI Case Files, Records of the National War Labor Board (World War II) (Record Group 202), National Archives, Federal Records Center, Suitland, Maryland; interview with Byron Buchholz.

4. For wartime wage trends nationally, see Seidman, *American Labor,* ch. 7, and Lichtenstein, "Industrial Unionism," esp. chs. 4–6.

5. A copy of the 1940 settlement, dated December 27, 1940, is in AFL-Series 7. Also, MB, November 29 and December 27, 1940.

Negotiations and results of the 1941 settlement are revealed in USCS Records, File 196-6124, esp. B. M. Marshman, USCS Commissioner, Final Report, August 16, 1941. On overtime: MB, January 2, 1945.

6. On factory conditions: interviews with William Skaar and Byron Buchholz and letter from Skaar to the author, August 1, 1975. See also Gordon Haferbecker, *Wisconsin Labor Laws* (Madison: University of Wisconsin Press, 1958), p. 30. There are many grievances filed on union forms in FLU 19587 Papers, Box 6.

7. The strengthening of centralized leadership was a national phenomenon during the war. See Seidman, *American Labor,* and Lichtenstein, "Industrial Unionism." Direct evidence of this pattern in 19587's affairs is fragmentary but appears, e.g., in USCS Records, Files 196–6124 and 300–2594, and in NWLB Records, Case No. 111–581–D and Case No. 111–15754–HD, as well as MB, esp. February 11, 1944, and January 2, 1945, and in interviews with Byron Buchholz, Max Onsager, and Evelyn Gotzion. Also conference of Federal Labor Unions of Wisconsin, *Proceedings* (meeting held in Madison, March 14–15, 1942; pamphlet, SHSW).

8. Election of 1939: MB, December 1, 1939, January 8, 1940. Biemiller's activities: Biemiller reports, February 20, 24, 1941, organizers' reports, WSFL Papers, Box 5. Turnover in leadership: MB, 1941–45, passim, esp. September 9, 27, December 9, 1944, January 10, February 10, 1945. Sergeants-at-Arms: MB, January 30, 1940. Motion against propaganda, etc.: MB, January 16, 1942. Rumors of 1945 and charges: MB, August 2, 1945. Receivership: MB, December 8, 1945. Also, interviews with Evelyn Gotzion, Pat Lowe, John Stromski.

9. See Lichtenstein, "Industrial Unionism," esp. ch. 11.

10. On the controversy, interviews with Evelyn Gotzion, Max Onsager, Pat Lowe, and John Stromski. Also MB, January 13, March 10, 27, April 21, 1945.

11. MB, late 1944–early 1945, passim.

12. This paragraph is somewhat speculative. These tendencies conform to national patterns. Interviews and MB references make it clear that internal conflict was intense and often personal and that, aside from the IAM matter, it invoked little in the way of ideology or even bargaining strategy differences.

13. Interview with Max Onsager; USCS Records, File 196-6124, esp. B. M. Marshman, Final Report, August 4, 1941.

14. Bertha Sime, Recording Secretary, to Leroy Berigan, December 22, 1942; union contract proposals in report by NWLB Tri-partite Panel, June 3, 1943, NWLB Records, Case No. 111–581–D.

15. Statement and brief of Ray-O-Vac Company, ca. March 20, 1943; David Sigman to Leroy Berigan, February 19, 1943; Berigan to FLU 19587 Grievance Committee, February 18, 1943; Harry Malcolm, NWLB Special Representative, memo, ca. April 12, 1943; Patrick Rogers, AFL Representative, brief, April 15, 1943, all in ibid.

16. James B. Holmes, Preliminary Report and Progress Report, both dated February 19, 1943, USCS Records, File 300–2594.

17. Synopsis, ca. February 22, 1943, transferring case from USCS to NWLB; statement and brief of Ray-O-Vac Company, ca. March 20, 1943; Leroy Berigan to Grievance Committee, February 18, 1943, and to David Sigman, February 22, 1943, all in NWLB Records, Case No. 111–581–D.

18. James B. Holmes to Leroy Berigan, Febuary 18, 1943, and February 23, 1943, ibid.

19. On the activities of the National War Labor Board during World War II, see Seidman, *American Labor from Defense to Reconversion,* esp. pp. 81–86, 91, 109–30, 145–49. Company perceptions that the board functioned to embolden the union are found in company brief, n.d., but ca. April 1943, NWLB Records, Case No. 111–581–D. Malcolm's observations are contained in his memo ca. April 12, 1943, ibid.

20. Tri-partite Panel report, June 3, 1943; Meyer Kastenbaum, chairman of tri-partite panel, to Henrietta Shaw, April 30, 1943; John O. Levinson, NWLB Assistant Director of Disputes, to members of Region VI Regional Labor Board, July 23, 1943, in ibid.

21. Leroy Berigan to Meyer Kastenbaum, May 4, 1943; Patrick Rogers telegram to Kastenbaum, May 10; Ralph E. Axley, attorney for Ray-O-Vac, to Kastenbaum, May 13, ibid.

22. Ray-O-Vac brief, ca. June 1945; Ray-O-Vac petition for reconsideration, ca. November 20, 1945, in NWLB Records, Case No. 111–15754–HO. The acerbic comments, by Vice-president Leroy Berigan, appear in his comment on report by Hearing Officer, ca. July 1, 1945, ibid. The frustrations of unionists are seen in Al Breitzke, president of FLU 19587, to Harry Malcolm, April 8, 1943, ibid., Case No. 111–581–D, and in the communications by NWLB Special Representative Malcolm and USCS Commissioner Holmes previously cited.

23. Interviews with Max Onsager and Byron Buchholz; MB, December 8, 1945.

VII. FLU 19587 AND THE POSTWAR ERA

1. MB, March 9, 1946.

2. Seidman, *American Labor,* pp. 213–69, and Frank Emspak, "The Break-up of the Congress of Industrial Organizations (CIO), 1945–1950" (Ph.D. dissertation, University of Wisconsin, 1972). See also the works by Markowitz, Hamby, Mills, Slichter, and Lee cited in Bibliographical Essay at the end of this book, as well as Barton J. Bernstein, "The Truman Administration and the Steel Strike of 1946," *Journal of American History* 52 (March 1966): 791–803.

3. In September 1945, for example, "1500 good militant members" of Federal Labor Union 18456, Simmons Furniture, Kenosha, struck with eventual AFL sanction. (J. F. Friedrick to William Green, October

17, 1945; Green to Gregory Wallig, October 19, 1945; Wallig to Green, November 30, 1945; Papers of FLU 18456, AFL-Series 7.) *Union Labor News,* September 1947, p. 1; David M. Oshinsky, *Senator Joseph McCarthy and the American Labor Movement* (Columbia: University of Missouri Press, 1976), pp. 16–35.

4. The reports of WSFL organizers for 1946 and 1947 (WSFL Papers, Box 7) reflect the atmosphere of crisis and controversy in the ranks of labor after the war, as well as the bitterness of the struggle for control of the state labor movement between AFL and CIO forces.

5. Grievances dating from the period December 1945 through 1948 appear in FLU 19587 Papers, Box 6. The Grievance Committee's complaint is in Max Onsager to Personnel Manager S. L. Rorge, November 11, 1947, ibid.

6. Interviews with Max Onsager and Evelyn Gotzion; MB, November 11, 1947. For a sociological profile of the shop steward, see Sidney Peck, *The Rank-and-File Leader* (New Haven, Conn.: College and University Press, 1963). FLU 19587's stewards seem partially to fit Peck's model, although there is little evidence that they were as class conscious as his account suggests as being typical (pp. 320–41).

7. The 1947 contract pledged the union to "actively assist the Management" in maintaining discipline and efficiency and described this provision as "the essence of this contract." (Agreement dated April 15, 1947, FLU 19587 Papers, Box 6.)

8. Peck, *Rank-and-File Leader,* pp. 31–32; interview with William Skaar. The quote is in David Sigman to Frank Fenton, December 26, 1939, AFL-Series 7. Over the years, the cumbersomeness of AFL procedures and the federation representatives' inability or unwillingness to respond to the shop-level problems of federal unionists was a major point of criticism among the latter. Generally, however, interviewees recall AFL service for 19587 as prompt and helpful; some of those interviewed, such as Max Onsager, viewed much shop-level disagreement as primarily the product of workers' pettiness and impetuousness. In general, too, the AFL and WSFL representatives who serviced 19587, such as David Sigman, J. F. Friedrick, and Charles Heymanns, enjoyed the respect and even the affection of local union members. The log of organizers' activities, 1940–50, in WSFL Papers, Boxes 5–8, indicates that, whatever the quality of service rendered, the federal labor unions, including 19587, were by no means neglected by staff representatives.

9. Charles Heymanns report, July 30, 1949; J. F. Friedrick report, August 31, 1949, organizers' reports, WSFL Papers, 1949, Box 8.

10. AFL report, March 25, 1946, enclosed in J. F. Friedrick to FLU 19587 secretary-treasurer, Ira Bailey, March 28, 1946, FLU 19587 Papers, Box 6; copy of letter from Melvin Krantzler, UE District 11 research director, to Phil Smith, UE representative, Milwaukee, November 23, 1948, with Smith note to Skaar at bottom of page, ibid.

11. MB, February 19, 1946; Arvel Kinney, USCS Commissioner, Progress Report, April 24, 1946, USCS Records, File 466-0401; J. F. Friedrick to William Green, April 24, 1946, AFL-Series 7; typescript of radio speech produced by the National Association of Manufacturers, read by A. M. Polland of Ray-O-Vac, February 23, 1948, FLU 19587 Papers, Box 6.

12. MB, December 1945–May 1946; USCS Records, File 466-0401; Max Onsager to William Green, April 3, 1946; Green to J. F. Friedrick, April 11, 1946; Friedrick to Green, April 24, 1946; Green to Friedrick (telegram), April 30, 1946; Friedrick to Green, May 10, 1946; Onsager to Green, May 10, 1946, all in AFL-Series 7. The quoted words of Friedrick are in his April 24 letter to Green. Interviews with William Skaar and Max Onsager. It should be recalled that 1945–46 was a time of bitter wage negotiations in basic production industries. Workers in steel, electrical appliances, and autos demanded increases of twenty-five cents an hour (around 30 percent). Settlements made in these industries, sometimes after prolonged strikes, were generally in the neighborhood of eighteen or nineteen cents. See Ronald Filippelli, "The United Electrical, Radio and Machine Workers of America, 1933–1949: The Struggle for Control" (Ph.D. dissertation, Pennsylvania State University, 1970), pp. 134–35.

13. *Union Labor News,* March 1947, p. 1.

14. J. F. Friedrick report, February 17, 1947; Charles Heymanns report, March 31, 1948, organizers' reports, WSFL Papers, Boxes 7 and 8 respectively.

15. On 1947 dispute: William Skaar and Max Onsager to Secretary of Labor Lewis Schwellenbach, February 24, 1947; Skaar to Florence Carlson, May 28, 1947; typescript of agreement, April 15, 1947, all in FLU 19587 Papers, Box 6. Also Arvel W. Kinney, Final Report, April 14, 1947, USCS Records, File 476–0150. On 1948 dispute: Skaar telegram to William Green, April 8, 1948; J. F. Friedrick to Green, April 12, 1948; Green to Skaar and to Friedrick, April 13, 1948, AFL-Series 7. Also John H. Behymer and James A. Despins, USCS Commissioners, Final Report, May 17, 1948, and other related reports in USCS Records, File 486-0207. Behymer used the word "futile" in his Progress Report of May 3, 1948. Evelyn Gotzion made her comments about reception of the contracts in a phone conversation with me, June 13, 1976.

16. Interview with William Skaar. There are many communications and reports in FLU 19587 Papers, Box 6, that discuss the diversity of unionization in the battery trade. See, e.g., Nat Spero, research director, United Electrical, Radio, and Machinery workers, to Phil Smith, August 17, 1948; mimeographed "Minutes of semi-annual conference of Delegates of AFL Dry Cell Battery Workers' Unions ...," Milwaukee, December 11–12, 1948; and Paul Parkhill to Skaar, January 15, 1949.

17. Virtually all the interviewees commented about the AFL's desire to turn FLU 19587 over to the IAM. Max Onsager's words quoted here appear in MB, February 10, 1948. Gregory Wallig's interview stressed AFL fear of alienating federal unionists and perhaps driving them into the arms of CIO unions.

18. Various battery councils and battery conferences had been formed, meeting sporadically, since the mid-1930s. Some enjoyed explicit AFL sanction; others were informal gatherings organized by the local unions. Over the years, 19587 members had kept in touch, through the mails and through personal visits, with battery workers throughout the Middle West. The Battery Workers' Conference of the late 1940s, however, was a more formally organized body than any previous such effort and had explicit AFL endorsement. The AFL attitude is implicit in its approach to organization, especially after ca. 1940. Skaar discussed the battery conference effort in my interview with him. In addition to the battery conference minutes cited in note 16 above, there are many references to periodic battery conferences in organizers' reports, WSFL Papers, Boxes 7–8.

19. J. F. Friedrick to Harold Edman, November 9, 1948; "Minutes . . . AFL . . . Battery workers' . . . Conference," December 11–12, 1948, FLU 19587 Papers, Box 6; MB, July 12, September 5, 1947; interview with William Skaar.

20. J. F. Friedrick reports, August 13–October 7, 1948, passim, organizers' reports, WSFL Papers, 1948, Box 8; Friedrick reports, April 5–15, 1949, ibid.; Friedrick report, December 13, 1949, ibid.; organizer Arthur A. Rabe report, December 12–13, 1949, ibid. On the UE, see Filippelli, "The United Electrical, Radio and Machine Workers."

21. Organizers' reports, 1946–50, passim, WSFL Papers, Boxes 7–8; interviews with William Skaar, Evelyn Gotzion, and Gregory Wallig.

22. Goulden, *Meany*, pp. 165–66; Arthur Goldberg, *AFL-CIO: Labor United* (New York: McGraw-Hill, 1956), pp. 120–21.

23. Interviews with William Skaar, Max Onsager, and Mrs. Lawrence Grab; Conference of Federal Labor Union of Wisconsin, *Proceedings*, March 14–15, 1942.

24. Interview with Gregory Wallig. Wallig served for serveral years as chairman of the Federal Labor Union Conference of Wisconsin. Edward E. Edwards, secretary, steering committee, Wisconsin FLUs, to all Wisconsin Federal Labor Unions, September 27, 1946, FLU 19587 Papers, Box 6. Wallig has in his possession the mimeographed minutes and other documents pertaining to postwar Wisconsin FLU activities. Related documents appear in WSFL Papers, Box 2.

25. Statement of purposes (hand dated March 15, 1952) is in Gregory Wallig's possession, as is a brief entitled "Federal Labor Unions — 1948."

26. Interview with David Sigman; J. F. Friedrick's remarks, Minutes

of FLU Conference meeting, Milwaukee, December 20, 1947, WSFL Papers, Box 2; report by federal labor union delegates to the 1947 AFL Convention, San Francisco, given to FLU Conference delegates, December 20, 1947, ibid.

27. Gregory Wallig to William Green, January 11, 1952, and reply, January 15, 1952, AFL Papers, Office of the President, William Green, 1924–52, Box 9; Minutes of Federal Labor Union Conference, October 29, 1955; Minutes of Federal Labor Union Conference, November 20, 1957, both in Wallig's possession. Estimates of federal labor union membership in Wisconsin, in addition to the figures given in these minutes, can be extrapolated from, e.g., Wisconsin State Federation of Labor, *Officers' Reports and Executive Board Meetings* [in lieu of convention proceedings] (Milwaukee, 1945), pp. 100–21; WSFL, *Proceedings of the fifty-eighth Annual Convention . . .* (Milwaukee, 1950), pp. 332–42; and Wisconsin State AFL-CIO, *Proceedings of the Third Biennial Convention* (Milwaukee, 1964), pp. 175–91.

28. Wisconsin State Federation of Labor, *Proceedings of the Fifty-eighth Annual Convention of the Wisconsin Federation of Labor* (Milwaukee, 1950), pp. 332–42, and *Proceedings of the Sixty-third Annual Convention . . .* (Milwaukee, 1955), pp. 172–83; report by federal labor union delegates to the 1947 AFL Convention, San Francisco, ca. December 20, 1947. Data on Wisconsin FLU representation are found in the roster of delegates that appears at the beginning of each annual report of AFL convention proceedings. The 1947 resolution appears in American Federation of Labor, *Report on the Proceedings of the Sixty-sixth Annual Convention . . .* (Washington, D.C., 1947), pp. 37–38, 479; the 1949 resolution is in *Proceedings of the Sixty-eighth Annual Convention. . .* (Washington, D.C., 1949), pp. 37–38.

29. MB, June 14, 1947; William Skaar and Marion White to Edward Edwards, September 20, 1947, FLU 19587 Papers, Box 6.

30. AFL, *Proceedings of the Sixty-sixth Annual Convention*, pp. 482, 506, and *Proceedings of the Sixty-eighth Annual Convention*, pp. 37–38, 478–79; William Green to George Haberman, president, WSFL, September 14, 1948, enclosed in Haberman to Skaar, October 1, 1948; Orla Coleman and Marion White to George Meany, November 2, 1948, FLU 19587 Papers, Box 6; interviews with Mrs. Lawrence Grab, Max Onsager, and Evelyn Gotzion.

31. Interview with William Skaar; James White, vice-president Wisconsin Industrial Union Council (CIO), to Skaar, May 22 (1948?); Sanborn Dill to Skaar, August 20, 1948; Nat Spero to Phil Smith, August 17, 1948; copy of letter from Melvin Krantzler, UE District 11 research director, to Phil Smith, November 23, 1948 (letter was apparently resent from Smith to Skaar); and similar communications in FLU 19587 Papers, Box 6. Skaar also attempted to resurrect the progressive political activities that he and Lochner had sponsored in the 1930s. Under his direction, the union issued a newsletter several times

each month. "I feel that this little paper is an excellent way to educate our membership [as] to the economic conditions which . . . affect them." Skaar to Dill, December 18, 1947, FLU 19587 Papers, Box 6. No copies of the newsletter survive.

32. Interview with William Skaar.

33. Max Onsager to S. L. Rorge, November 11, 1947, FLU 19587 Papers, Box 6.

34. Copy of Wisconsin Employment Relations Board Certification statement, August 1, 1946, ibid.; NLRB election tally of ballots, March 30, 1948 (case no. 31–UA–46), ibid.

35. Interview with William Skaar.

EPILOGUE

1. Factual material in this epilogue derives largely from the interviews with Max Onsager, William Skaar, Evelyn Gotzion, and Mrs. Lawrence Grab. Also helpful were interviews with David Sigman and Gregory Wallig, as well as a conversation with UAW Local 1329's current president, Elmer Davis, January 7, 1975. The Madison *Capital-Times* covers the 1956 strike (May 17–June 22, 1956). The *Union Labor News* is available in microfilm form and contains much helpful information on the fifties, sixties, and early seventies. I am indebted to Mr. and Mrs. John Stromski and to Marion Shaw for recollections and newspaper clippings of the battery workers' first strike.

Bibliographical Essay

Manuscript collections and personal interviews have provided the bulk of the information for this study. The records of Federal Labor Union 19587 are housed at the State Historical Society of Wisconsin in Madison. They are extremely rich and rewarding and do credit to the men and women whose names and activities are chronicled therein. In addition, there are significant materials relating to the union in the AFL Papers, Series 7, Strikes and Agreements File, also at the State Historical Society. These AFL records contain the reports and correspondence pertaining to federal labor unions and are a source of great importance for the study of those directly affiliated organizations, as well as the AFL itself. Assorted materials relating to the battery industry and to the federal labor unions appear in the Industry Reference Files and in the William Green Papers, Series 4 and 11D respectively, of the AFL Papers. The Papers of the Wisconsin State Federation of Labor contain scattered correspondence and clippings reflective of the atmosphere of the 1930s; minutes and resolutions pertaining to the state's federal labor unions; and weekly reports of organizers, from the period 1940 to 1950. Gregory Wallig of Kenosha supplied copies of FLU Conference minutes and related materials not found in the WSFL Papers. I also consulted materials relating to FLU 19587 in the files of the United States Conciliation Service (Record Group 280), the National Labor Relations Board (Record Group 25), and the National War Labor Board (World War II) (Record Group 202). These materials are housed at the Federal Records Center in Suitland, Maryland. They contain contracts, briefs, statistical information, and other valuable material concerning labor-management relations. The USCS and NWLB records are particularly useful in tracing the company's position.

In January 1975, I interviewed veterans of 19587's early years. Most of the conversations took place in their homes in and around Madison. In addition, I talked at length on the telephone with William Skaar during the same month. In selecting interviewees, I initially contacted men and women whose names appeared prominently in the union's records and who were still living in the Madison area. Many of these people preferred that I talk with others whom they thought better informed about union affairs. In the end, the primary consideration in choosing interviewees was the willingness of the people to talk with me. Upon reflection, I am satisfied that I consulted a representative spectrum of unionists, whose comments reflected the various viewpoints appearing in documentary records. In the course of these interviews I also spoke with other people — the spouses of 19587 members — who had worked elsewhere in the city and who had been active in the local labor movement. In June 1976, I had extensive conversations with David Sigman, regional director of the AFL from 1937 through 1945, and with Gregory Wallig, an active member of FLU 18456, president of this local union between 1946 and 1952, and for over twenty years after an organizer on the AFL staff. Listed below are the names, dates, and circumstances of the interviews cited in the notes to this book:

Mr. and Mrs. John Stromski, at their home in Monona, Wisconsin, January 6, 1975

Marion Shaw, at the Stromski home, January 6, 1975

Pat Lowe, at his apartment in Madison, January 6, 1975

Evelyn Gotzion, at the Park Motor Inn coffee shop, Madison, January 6, 1975

Mrs. Lawrence Grab, at her home in Madison, January 7, 1975

Byron Buchholz, at his home in Madison, January 7, 1975

Max Onsager, at his home in Madison, January 7, 1975

Elmer Davis, at UAW Local 1329 headquarters, 2435 East Washington Street, Madison, January 7, 1975

William Skaar, telephone interview while he was at home in Bradenton, Florida, January 15, 1975

David Sigman, at his home in Shorewood, Wisconsin, June 13, 1976

Gregory Wallig, at his home in Kenosha, Wisconsin, June 13, 1976

Evelyn Gotzion, telephone conversation while she was at home in Madison, June 13, 1976.

The people I talked with were well informed, and their

memories squared impressively with the written record. Wherever possible I have checked recollections against documentary material. I have extensive notes, written immediately after each interview, in my possession. I did not record the conversations.

Two other primary sources provided useful information. The *Union Labor News*, published in Madison from 1937 onward, contains many references to FLU 19587 and has valuable material on living and working conditions in Madison, local politics, and unionism in Wisconsin. In addition, the State Historical Society has a complete run of the Ray-O-Vac employee association newsletter, 1919–29. I wrote several times requesting additional information from Ray-O-Vac about its personnel policies and employee relations activities, but the company did not answer my letters. Company policies and statements, however, appear frequently in the union's records and in the files of government agencies. In addition, several of the union veterans with whom I spoke enjoyed cordial relations with company officials and presented the company's view of various controversies with considerable sympathy. I also acquired access to a handful of company newsletters dating from the 1940s and 1950s. How more systematic access to Ray-O-Vac records might have changed this account I can only speculate. My primary concern was with the establishment and history of the union itself; thus, I did not feel that lack of company materials was critical.

Before leaving the subject of manuscript and documentary records, I should note that this monograph is a part of a broader inquiry into the American labor movement in the 1930s. In connection with this effort, I have examined numerous other manuscript collections, such as the AFL and CIO records at the State Historical Society of Wisconsin and at Catholic University and AFL-CIO headquarters, both in Washington, D.C. I have also gone through papers relating to the auto workers and other unions at Wayne State University in Detroit, the steelworkers and electrical workers at Pennsylvania State University, and the teamsters, pulp, sulphite workers, and other unions and individuals at the State Historical Society of Wisconsin. In addition, I have worked in several record groups at the National Archives and the Federal Records Center. Many of the general comments and contextual observations in this study of Federal Labor Union 19587 are based upon the impressions and evidence drawn from this research.

There are, of course, few published references to Federal Labor Union 19587. Indeed, the searcher will find disappointingly little material on the history of the labor movement in Madison, in Dane County, or even in the state of Wisconsin. Several monographs and unpublished works do provide background for the city and its economic and demographic characteristics. See Edgar Z. Palmer, *The Prewar Industrial Pattern of Wisconsin*, Wisconsin Commerce Studies (Madison: University of Wisconsin, 1947); John W. Alexander, *An Economic Base Study of Madison, Wisconsin* (Madison: University of Wisconsin, School of Commerce, Bureau of Research and Service, June 1953); Richard Skinner Allis, "Urban Redevelopment: Study of a Selected Area in Madison, Wisconsin" (M.S. thesis, University of Wisconsin, 1947), pp. 12–17; James Paul Collins, "Real Property and Low Income Area Survey of Madison, Wisconsin" (M.A. thesis, University of Wisconsin, 1941); and Calvert Lampert Dedrick, "Incomes and Occupations in Madison, Wisconsin" (Ph.D. dissertation, University of Wisconsin, 1933).

Information about Wisconsin labor is surprisingly scanty. Robert Nesbit, *Wisconsin: A History* (Madison: University of Wisconsin Press, 1973) is an intelligent introduction to the state but it has little on labor. Perhaps the forthcoming volumes by Paul Glad and E. David Cronin on Wisconsin in the twentieth century, part of a multivolume work on the Badger State, will yield additional material. Other published works of interest include Edwin E. Witte, "Labor in Wisconsin History," *Wisconsin Magazine of History* 35 (Winter 1951–52): 83–86, 137–42; David M. Oshinsky, "Wisconsin Labor and the Campaign of 1952," ibid., 56 (Winter 1972-73): 109–18; Oshinsky, *Senator Joseph McCarthy and the American Labor Movement* (Columbia: University of Missouri Press, 1976), esp. pp. 1–59; Gordon Haferbecker, *Wisconsin Labor Law* (Madison: University of Wisconsin Press, 1958); and Thomas W. Gavett, *Development of the Labor Movement in Milwaukee* (Madison: University of Wisconsin Press, 1965). Gavett's brief discussion of Wisconsin labor in the 1930s and 1940s contains the most helpful background information currently in print. Dissertations and theses help to fill in some of the gaps. Daniel Hershel Kruger, "A Study of Collective Bargaining in Wisconsin" (Ph.D. dissertation, University of Wisconsin, 1954) is frustrating because it deals almost exclusively in general conclusions. Useful in a broad way on such subjects as labor force characteristics, ethnic composition, education levels, and the like, his survey data, although they include Ray-O-Vac, are not broken down into specific companies. Robert W. Ozanne, "The Effects of Communist Leadership on American Trade Unions" (Ph.D. dissertation, University of Wisconsin, 1954) depicts some of the fervor and ideological conflict that shook Wisconsin labor in the 1930s and 1940s. Walter Uphoff, *Kohler on Strike: Thirty Years of Conflict* (Boston: Beacon Press, 1966) also contributes in this regard. Patrick Delmore, "The Kohler Strike of the 1930s" (M.S. thesis, University of Wisconsin — Stevens Point, 1975) examines the tribulations of another federal labor union. See also Paul Krakowski, "Press Treatment of Wisconsin Labor Issues, 1936–38" (M.A. thesis, University of Wisconsin, 1947). A series of sketches on leading personalities in the history of Wisconsin labor by Harold J. Newton in *Wisconsin Labor* (Milwaukee: Wisconsin State AFL-CIO, 1975–76) is highly informative. Robert Ozanne is currently writing a history of labor in Wisconsin, thus filling the need for a solid, comprehensive work on the state's working people and labor movement.

Local labor history in general has been sadly neglected. Local union records are often carelessly maintained and when available are frequently dwarfed by the records of national unions. The minute books and correspondence files of the locals are often rather prosaic, perhaps dissuading historians who long for the excitement of the great strikes or the high drama associated with the clash of famous personalities and vivid ideologies. Students of nineteenth-century labor history have done pioneering work in local union records, but their counterparts working with twentieth-century subjects have seldom followed suit.

Two recent studies of local unionism in the automobile industry help to redress the balance, however. John G. Kruchko, *The Birth of a Union Local: The History of UAW Local 674, Norwood, Ohio, 1933-1940* (Ithaca: New York State School of Industrial and Labor Relations, 1972) has the advantage of dealing with a local union that was in the thick of things during the auto workers' struggles in the 1930s. Kruchko, however, had little access to manuscript sources and had to rely almost exclusively on interviews. A valuable contribution to grass-roots labor history, it suffers from the author's unanalytical approach and from his decision to end his story before the coming of the war. Peter J. Friedlander, *The Emergence of a UAW Local, 1936-1939: A Study in Class and Cluture* (Pittsburgh: University of Pittsburgh

Press, 1975) also suffers from a limited time span and exclusive reliance on oral interviews. It is analytical, however, and suggests important questions about the nature of the labor uprising of the 1930s and the character of class consciousness in America. In addition, Friedlander's intensive interviewing techniques enable him to capture much of the flavor of working-class life in Detroit and Hamtramck in the 1930s. Claude E. Hoffman, *Sit-Down in Anderson: UAW Local 663, Anderson, Indiana* (Detroit: Wayne State University Press, 1968) is a firsthand account, of some limited use in the history of the UAW but no model for local union history.

Some of the personal histories cited below do contain vivid recollections of grass-roots organization, but this type of source is sporadic and incomplete, usually relegating activities in local unions to background material for the author's larger role in the labor movement. In addition to the works by James Matles and James Higgins, Wyndham Mortimer, and Alice Lynd and Staughton Lynd cited later, see Clayton W. Fountain, *Union Guy* (New York: Viking Press, 1949) and Frank Marquart, *An Auto Worker's Journal: The UAW from Crusade to One-party Union* (University Park: Pennsylvania State University Press, 1975), esp. pp. 40–101. The oral histories of UAW activists at Wayne State University and those of steelworker stalwarts at Pennsylvania State University also contribute to the record of local unionism in the 1930s and 1940s.

Much of the literature touching upon the important questions associated with local unionism — the nature of militancy, the conflict between ordinary workers and union bureaucracies, the place of the union in workers' lives — is the work of economists and sociologists. Ozanne's dissertation, cited earlier, is a detailed examination of UAW Local 248, Allis-Chalmers, Milwaukee, although its primary focus on the role of communists in the union limits its general interest. Some sociological work has been helpful to me in an indirect way, suggesting some of the patterns of responses to work, management, and unions prevalent among local unionists. Richly suggestive, although of course applicable to my work here only in the most general way, has been the series by John Goldthorpe, David Lockwood, Frank Bechhofer, and Jennifer Platt, *The Affluent Worker: Political Attitudes and Behavior, The Affluent Worker: Industrial Attitudes and Behavior,* and *The Affluent Worker in the Class Structure* (Cambridge, England: Cambridge University Press, 1968–69).

C. Wright Mills, *The New Men of Power: America's Labor Leaders* (New York: Harcourt Brace, 1948) describes well the pressures and inducements acting on labor leaders to encourage "statesmanship" especially during and after World War II. Sidney Peck, *The Rank-and-File Leader* (New Haven: College and University Press, 1963) delineates the characteristics of local stewards and activists. Many of his observations are applicable to at least the militant wing of FLU 19587. Frank Riessman, "Workers' Attitudes towards Participation and Leadership" (Ph.D. dissertation, Columbia University, 1955) is very helpful in grasping the patterns of aggressiveness and passivity among 19587's workers, as well as in understanding the importance of informal contacts and associations. Alvin Gouldner, *Wildcat Strikes: A Study in Worker-Management Relationships* (Yellow Springs, Ohio: Antioch Press, 1954) is illuminating on the subject of rank-and-file activism in crisis situations.

The best book on local unionism is Jack Barbash, *Labor's Grass Roots: A Study of the Local Union* (New York: Harper and Brothers, 1961). Much of the sociological literature on local unionisn is more disappointing than useful. Leonard Sayles and George Strauss, *The Local Union: Its Place in the Industrial Plant* (New York: Harper and Brothers, 1953) is disappointingly sketchy, while Joel Seidman et al., *The Worker Views His Union* (Chicago: University of Chicago Press, 1958) promises more hard evidence than it delivers. Other titles that touch on the relationship between workers and local unions unclude Paul E. Sultan, *The Disenchanted Unionist* (New York: Harper and Row, 1963); Arnold Tannenbaum and Robert L. Kahn, *Participation in Union Locals* (Evanston: Row, Peterson, 1958); and Arnold Rose, *Union Solidarity* (Minneapolis: University of Minnesota Press, 1952). The patient reader can glean from these sources some general impressions of commonly held working-class attitudes. Taken together, these works do stress the great importance of unions in the lives of their members, but none provides a penetrating assessment or a compelling analytical model on the subject.

Moving from local matters to the more general aspects of the labor movement is not quite so frustrating, but even here much work remains to be done. Even the basic history of the AFL is surprisingly spotty. Philip A. Taft's three volumes — *The A.F. of L. in the Time of Gompers* (New York: Harper and Brothers, 1957); *The A.F. of L.: From the Death of Gompers to the Merger* (New

York: Harper and Row, 1959); and *Organized Labor in American History* (New York: Harper and Row, 1964) — are essential, but they are frustrating and difficult to work with. They contain invaluable material from the AFL Executive Council minutes unobtainable elsewhere, but each of the books is idiosyncratic in organization and coverage. I found these volumes to have relatively little useful and compact material on the federal labor unions, for example. More valuable on this important subject are James O. Morris, *Conflict within the AFL: A Study of Craft versus Industrial Unionism, 1901–1938* (Ithaca: New York State School of Industrial and Labor Relations, 1958); Harry A. Millis and Royal Montgomery, *The Economics of Labor,* Organized Labor, vol. 3 (New York: McGraw-Hill, 1945); and, especially, Lewis L. Lorwin, *The American Federation of Labor: History, Policies, Prospects* (Washington, D.C.: Brookings Institution, 1933). Lorwin's work, though obviously dated, provides the clearest description in print of the AFL's structure, its various component bodies, and its mechanisms. This book has the best material available on such subjects as the national convention, the departments, the city centrals, and, of particular interest here, the federal labor unions. A model of organization, clarity, and comprehensiveness, it is an enduringly valuable book for students of the AFL. Of course, the *Reports of Proceedings* of the AFL's annual conventions must be consulted.

Three books by Irving Bernstein are basic for students of this period — *Lean Years: A History of the American Worker, 1920–1933* (Boston: Houghton Mifflin, 1960); *The Turbulent Years: A History of the American Worker, 1933–1941* (Boston: Houghton Mifflin, 1970); and *New Deal Collective Bargaining Policy* (Berkeley: University of California Press, 1950). Bernstein writes with deep understanding on such diverse subjects as labor legislation, welfare capitalism, the strikes and organizing campaigns of the 1930s, and the AFL-CIO split. His biographical vignettes of leading figures in the labor movement are an added feature. The verve and scope of the two general volumes should not dissuade students from consulting *New Deal Collective Bargaining Policy* as well, for despite its pedestrian title it stands on its own as a succinct introduction to labor and public policy in the early 1930s. The other major overview of the decade is Walter Galenson, *The CIO Challenge to the AFL: A History of the American Labor Movement, 1935–1941* (Cambridge, Mass.: Harvard University Press, 1960). A thorough, competent work of the institutional school, its attention is firmly riveted on major areas of trade union growth and conflict and on the AFL-CIO controversy. The Taft volumes previously cited supplement Galenson's treatment of organizational matters, the inner workings of the AFL, jurisdictional disputes, and similar topics. Those interested in the federal labor unions will find the best material in Bernstein, *Turbulent Years;* Morris, *Conflict within the AFL;* and Lorwin, *The American Federation of Labor.* Casting additional light on the societal limitations that impinged on the labor movement in the thirties and forties are Milton Derber, "The New Deal and Labor" and David Brody, "The New Deal and World War II," both in John Braeman, Robert H. Bremner, and David Brody, eds., *The National Level,* The New Deal, vol. 1 (Columbus: Ohio State University Press, 1975), pp. 110–32 and 267–309, respectively.

Bernstein's work on the 1920s remains the best survey of welfare capitalism. Robert Ozanne, *A Century of Labor-Management Relations at McCormick and International Harvester* (Madison: University of Wisconsin Press, 1967) is based on unique corporate records and contains a wealth of information on company unionism in the 1920s. Stuart Brandes, "Welfarism in American Industry, 1880–1940" (Ph.D. dissertation, University of Wisconsin, 1970), esp. pp. 91–100, 236–58, contains much material on welfare activities of the type that Ramsay and French Battery embarked on in the 1920s.

Fresh monographic literature on labor in the 1930s is disappointingly slow in appearing. Sidney Fine's two volumes on the automobile industry are models of narrative history — *The Automobile under the Blue Eagle: Labor, Management, and the Automobile Manufacturing Code* (Ann Arbor: University of Michigan Press, 1963) and *Sit-Down! The General Motors Strike of 1936–37* (Ann Arbor: University of Michigan Press, 1969). Daniel Leab's study of the Newspaper Guild, *A Union of Individuals: The Formation of the American Newspaper Guild* (New York: Columbia University Press, 1970), is competent and informative. John N. Schacht, "Toward Industrial Unionism: Bell Telephone Workers and Company Unions, 1919–1937," *Labor History* 16, no. 1 (Winter 1975): 5–36, sheds important light on a significant chapter in union development.

But many of the unions await their scholarly chroniclers. Those interested in the rubberworkers, for example, must rely on reminiscences published in the union's newspaper, and books and articles written in the 1930s and 1940s. Much the same is true with regard to the steelworkers, electrical workers, aluminum workers, and many other major CIO affiliates. There is little current monographic literature on the textile unions, the needle trades unions, the oil and refinery workers, the glass workers, and cement workers. Even key organizations such as the United Brotherhood of Carpenters and Joiners, the International Brotherhood of Teamsters, and the United Mine Workers have not had their activities in the 1930s and 1940s subjected to careful scholarly analysis. Such works as David Brody, *The Butcher Workmen: A Study in Unionization* (Cambridge, Mass.: Harvard University Press, 1964); Garth Mangum, *The Operating Engineers: The Economic Study of a Trade Union* (Cambridge, Mass.: Harvard University Press, 1964); Mark Perlman, *The Machinists: A New Study of American Trade Unionism* (Cambridge, Mass.: Harvard University Press, 1961); and Charles Larrowe, *Harry Bridges: The Rise and Fall of Radical Labor in the U.S.* (New York: Lawrence Hill, 1972) deal with this period usefully enough, but only as part of their respective institutional or biographical concerns. Dissertations fill some gaps. Donald Sofchalk, "The Little Steel Strike of 1937" (Ph.D. dissertation, Ohio State University, 1961) and William Haskett, "Ideological Radicals, the American Federation of Labor, and Federal Labor Policy in the Strikes of 1934" (Ph.D. dissertation, UCLA, 1957) are both superb. Irving Brotslaw, "Trade Unionism in the Pulp and Paper Industry" (Ph.D dissertation, University of Wisconsin, 1964) has much information on that subject. Ronald Filippelli, "The United Electrical, Radio and Machine Workers of America, 1933-1949: The Struggle for Control" (Ph.D. dissertation, Pennsylvania State University, 1970) focuses on internal developments in a union whose activities often touched the battery trade. In general, however, with the exception of the automobile industry, the reader of the appropriate chapters of Bernstein, *Turbulent Years* and Galenson, *CIO Challenge* will find the best available material on any given industry or unionizing effort.

Some of the most interesting and provocative literature dealing with the 1930s and 1940s has appeared in periodicals. The best introduction to current historiographical problems can be gained by reading David Brody, "Radical Labor History and Rank-and-File Militancy," *Labor History* 16, no. 1 (Winter 1975): 117–26; Brody, "Labor and the Great Depression: The Interpretive Prospects," ibid., 13, no. 2 (Spring 1972): 231–44; Brody, "Working Class History in the Great Depression [a review of Friedlander, *The Emergence of a UAW Local*]," *Reviews in American History* 4, no. 2 (June 1976): 262–67; and James Green, "Working Class Militancy in the Depression," *Radical America* 6, no. 6 (November–December 1972): 1–36. A series of articles and interviews by Staughton Lynd make the case for the radicalism inherent in working-class activism in the 1930s. See Lynd, ed., "Personal Histories of the Early CIO," ibid., 5, no. 3 (May–June 1971): 49–76; "The Possibility of Radicalism in the Early 1930s: The Case of Steel," ibid., 6, no. 6 (November–December 1972): 37–64; Lynd, "Guerrilla History in Gary," *Liberation* 14, no. 7 (October 1969): 17–21; and Alice Lynd and Staughton Lynd, eds., *Rank and File: Personal Histories by Working Class Organizers* (Boston: Beacon Press, 1972). Lorin Lee Cary, "Institutionalized Conservatism in the Early C.I.O.: Adolph Germer, a Case Study," *Labor History* 13, no. 4 (Fall 1972): 475–504, lends support to the thesis that rank-and-file militancy suffered at the hands of labor's bureaucratic impulses.

In addition to the interviews and personal histories compiled by the Lynds, there is a great deal of memoir literature on the 1930s. Most of the recent publications in this category reinforce the heroic image of the decade and decry the current complacency of organized labor. Forceful examples include Len De Caux, *Labor Radical: From the Wobblies to the CIO – a Personal History* (Boston: Beacon Press, 1970), Farrel Dobbs, *Teamster Rebellion* (New York: Monad Press, 1972) and *Teamster Power* (New York: Monad Press, 1973); James Matles and James Higgins, *Them and Us: Struggles of a Rank-and-File Union* (Englewood Cliffs, N.J.: Prentice-Hall, 1974); and Wyndham Mortimer, *Organize! My Life as a Union Man* (Boston: Beacon Press, 1971). Intelligent, briskly written syntheses of this theme are found in Jeremy Brecher, *Strike!* (San Francisco: Straight Arrow Books, 1972) and Art Preis, *Labor's Giant Step: Twenty Years of the CIO,* 2d ed. (New York: Pathfinder Press, 1972).

Scholarly literature on labor in the Second World War is sharply limited and as yet forms little basis for synthesis. Joel Seidman's *American Labor from Defense to Reconversion* (Chicago: University of Chicago Press, 1953) is still standard and is an excellent introduction, especially in view of the limited materials available to the author. The Brecher and Preis works cited above contain vivid, though likely overstated, accounts of rank-and-file protest versus government and union bureaucracies during the war years. All three works carry the story through the strike-torn period of 1945 and 1946. The Preis book also takes a critical look at organized labor's enlistment in the postwar anticommunist crusade. Nelson Nauen Lichtenstein, "Industrial Unionism under the No-strike Pledge: A Study of the CIO during the Second World War" (Ph.D. dissertation, University of California, Berkeley, 1974) and Frank Emspak, "The Break-up of the Congress of Industrial Organizations (CIO), 1945–1950" (Ph.D. dissertation, University of Wisconsin, 1972) cast important light on wartime and postwar developments. Articles by Lichtenstein, James Green, and Ed Jennings highlight *Radical America* 9, no. 4–5 (July–August 1975), a special issue dealing with labor during World War II. Two excellent, if contrasting, assessments of labor policy during the war are found in Brody, "The New Deal and World War II," in Braeman, Bremner, and Brody, eds., *The National Level,* The New Deal, vol. 1, pp. 267–309; and Paul A. C. Koistinen, "Mobilizing the World War II Economy: Labor and the Industrial-Military Alliance," *Pacific Historical Review* 42, no. 4 (November 1973): 443–78.

Something of the sense of hope and fear concerning labor influence after the war can be seen in such works as Mills, *The New Men of Power* (previously cited); Norman D. Markowitz, *The Rise and Fall of the People's Century: Henry A. Wallace and American Liberalism, 1941–1948* (New York: Free Press, 1973), esp. pp. 126, 137, 153; Alonzo Hamby, *Beyond the New Deal: Harry S. Truman and American Liberalism* (New York: Columbia University Press, 1973), esp. pp. 34, 69, 154–56; Irving Howe and B. J. Widick, *The UAW and Walter Reuther* (New York: Random House, 1949), pp. 126–48; Frank Cormier and William J. Eaton, *Reuther* (Englewood Cliffs, N.J.: Prentice-Hall, 1970), pp. 218–30; Sumner H. Slichter, *The Challenge of Industrial Relations: Trade Unions, Management, and the Public Interest* (Ithaca, N.Y.: Cornell University Press, 1947), esp. ch. 6; and R. Alton Lee, *Truman and Taft-Hartley: A Question of Mandate* (Lexington: University of Kentucky Press, 1966), pp. 8–48.

The literature on communism in the unions is badly dated and needs revision, especially through grass-roots research. See, for example, Max Kampelman, *The Communist Party vs. the CIO: A Study in Power Politics* (New York: Praeger, 1957) and Ozanne, "The Effects of Communist Leadership on American Trade

Unions," previously cited, for traditional views. James R. Prick-
ett, "Communism and Factionalism in the United Automobile
Workers, 1939–1947," *Science and Society* 32, no. 3 (Summer
1968): 257–77, and the dissertations by Emspak and Filippelli
previously cited supply other perspectives.

Finally, in attempting to gain a grasp of the broad pattern of
American labor development over this crucial decade and a half,
several essays by David Brody, in addition to those previously
noted, are essential — "The Emergence of Mass-production
Unionism," in John Braeman, Robert H. Bremner, and Everett
Walters, eds., *Change and Continuity in Twentieth Century America*
(New York: Harper Torchbook, 1964), pp. 221–62; "The
Expansion of the American Labor Movement: Institutional
Sources of Stimulus and Restraint," in Stephen E. Ambrose, ed.,
Institutions in Modern America: Innovation in Structure and Process
(Baltimore: Johns Hopkins University Press, 1967), pp. 11–36;
and "The Rise and Decline of Welfare Capitalism," in Braeman,
Bremner, and Brody, eds., *Change and Continuity in Twentieth-
century America: The 1920s* (Columbus: Ohio State University
Press, 1968), pp. 146–78. Brody's thorough knowledge of the
history of American unionism and his willingness to ask difficult
questions make his work unusually penetrating and suggestive.

Index